# The Courier-Journal & Times
# COOKBOOK

## By LILLIAN MARSHALL

### Including 91 Favorite Cissy Gregg Recipes and 61 Photographs in Full Color

FIRST EDITION

FIRST PRINTING

COPYRIGHT 1971 BY THE COURIER-JOURNAL

AND LOUISVILLE TIMES CO. ALL RIGHTS RESERVED.

PRINTED IN THE U.S.A. BY STANDARD GRAVURE CORP.,

LOUISVILLE, KY.

# FOREWORD

Perhaps a food editor's greatest joy is the happy response from readers. Over the years as food editor of The Courier-Journal & Times Magazine, I have found that the happiest response has been to dishes that somehow have remained regional favorites.

This is what this book is all about. I have chosen the menus and recipes that have been requested time and again as treasured clippings have become faded or lost. Many of the recipes have been gleaned from the archive of good eating compiled by the late Cissy Gregg, my predecessor as Food Editor. Cissy's gaiety, her light-hearted approach to cooking and fine foods, piqued the imagination of two generations of cooks, including mine. You will find Cissy Gregg's recipes specially marked throughout the book.

Because many foods are associated with certain times of the year, the menus and recipes have been grouped into five divisions: Spring, Summer, Fall, Winter, and a section for Christmas. But good eating knows no season, and many people love the same foods in September as they did in May.

The recipes and pictures—all from the Magazine—illustrate my vision of what food should be: A double feast, first to the eye, then to the palate.

As food editor, and in the production of this cookbook, I have been fortunate to have had the aid of Thelma White, assistant and friend to both Cissy Gregg and to me.

One thing to keep in mind: There is nothing esoteric about the preparation of good food. Read, then, cook and enjoy!

*Lillian Marshall*

Louisville, Kentucky, 1971

# CONTENTS

● **A Cissy Gregg Special**

# Berry-Good Eating

Now for that annual springtime treat and calorie-counter's friend, the home-grown strawberry. A whole cupful of fresh strawberries comes to only 56 calories. But for a fling at letting calories fall where they may, here are strawberry desserts and marmalade!

### Strawberry-Cheese Pie Glacé

Baked 9-inch pie shell
1 8-ounce package cream cheese,
    softened to room temperature
3 tablespoons heavy cream
1 tablespoon sugar
1 teaspoon lemon juice
1 quart strawberries
1 cup red currant jelly
1 tablespoon hot water
1 tablespoon kirsch
For garnish (optional): 1 cup heavy cream, whipped
    and flavored with a little sugar and a tablespoon
    kirsch.

Whip the cream cheese with the 3 tablespoons cream, the sugar and lemon juice. Spread in bottom of pie shell and chill. Arrange strawberries, washed and dried, over the cheese layer, stem ends down. Prepare the glaze: Melt the jelly with the hot water over low heat, stirring until it foams up. Add the kirsch and allow to cool somewhat. Spoon warm glaze over strawberries and chill before serving.

### Strawberry Freeze

1 1/2 sticks butter
1 1/2 cups flour
1/2 cup brown sugar
1/2 cup chopped nutmeats
2 egg whites, beaten
1 cup sugar
2 cups sliced strawberries
2 tablespoons lemon juice
1 cup heavy cream, whipped
Whole berries for garnish

Melt butter in a pan about 9-inches square or 7- by 11-inches. Add flour, brown sugar and chopped nuts and spread evenly over the bottom of the pan. Place in 350-degree oven and bake 20 minutes, stirring every 5 minutes, making crumbs. Take out 1/2 cup crumbs and leave the rest in pan.

Beat the egg whites and gradually add the cup sugar, add the strawberries and lemon juice, beating until fluffy. Fold in the whipped cream. Pour mixture over the crumbs in the pan and sprinkle with the reserved 1/2 cup crumbs. Freeze overnight. Cut in squares; garnish each with a whole berry. Serves 8 or 9.

### Fresh Strawberry Cake

3 cups sifted cake flour
2 teaspoons baking powder
1 1/2 cups sugar
1 1/2 teaspoons salt
1 cup soft butter
4 eggs
2/3 cup milk
2 teaspoons vanilla
1 cup fresh strawberries, chopped
1/2 cup finely chopped walnuts

Sift flour, baking powder, sugar and salt together. Add butter, 2 of the eggs, milk and vanilla. Beat until blended. Add remaining 2 eggs. Beat well. Fold in strawberries and nuts. Turn into well-greased, 9-inch tube pan. Bake in moderate oven (375 degrees) 1 hour and 15 minutes, or until cake tests done. Cool. Drizzle Strawberry Glaze (recipe follows) over cake.

*Strawberry Glaze*

1 egg yolk, beaten
1 tablespoon soft butter or margarine
1 1/2 cups sifted confectioners' sugar
1/2 cup fresh strawberries, crushed

Combine egg yolk, butter and sugar, beating until blended. Add crushed berries and blend to a creamy consistency.

### Strawberry Marmalade

1 quart strawberries, sliced
2 large oranges
2 large lemons
6 cups sugar

Wash oranges and lemons and cut them into eighths. Remove seeds and grind fruit coarsely, rind and all. Add 1 cup of the sugar and let stand overnight. Bring to boiling, reduce heat and simmer, stirring frequently, for 40 minutes.

Add sliced berries and another cup of sugar. Simmer slowly, stirring frequently, for 20 minutes. Add remaining sugar and boil 6 minutes, stirring constantly—it scorches easily. Add a couple of drops of red food coloring at the end of the cooking period. Remove from heat, then skim and stir for 5 minutes. Pack in hot, sterilized jelly glasses. Cover with paraffin for storing; refrigerate for short-term use.

# Tax Bite? Try Pasta!

Judging from the lamentations that fill the air around the middle of April, it would appear that everything but the grocery bill has been mailed off to the Internal Revenue Service. As an economy dinner at tax time, pastas are rib-sticking and delicious.

## Five-Cheese Spaghetti

1 pound vermicelli spaghetti
2 teaspoons butter
2 teaspoons Worcestershire sauce
3/4 teaspoon dry mustard
1 small clove garlic, minced
1 cup sharp cheddar cheese, shredded
1 cup Swiss cheese, shredded
1 cup dry grated Parmesan (or mixed Parmesan-Romano)
1 small roll smoky cheese, shredded
1 cup Provolone cheese, shredded
Salt and pepper to taste
3 tablespoons butter
Paprika to taste
1 quart milk

Cook the spaghetti in plenty of rapidly boiling, salted water until just not quite tender. Drain. Shred all cheeses and toss them together. Butter a 3- or 4-quart casserole and sprinkle the Worcestershire sauce, mustard and minced garlic on the bottom. Place a layer of spaghetti in casserole, season lightly with salt, paprika and pepper, and dot with butter. Follow with a generous layer of the mixed cheeses. Make 3 layers each of spaghetti and cheeses, seasoning as indicated. Pour 1 quart of cold milk over all, cover and place in 350-degree oven.

Bake until hot through. Remove cover and, with fork and spoon, lift spaghetti from bottom to top. Cover, return to oven, wait 1/2 hour and repeat lifting. If it seems to be at all dry, add a little milk. Bake another 15 minutes, then lift again. The finished product should be creamy, not browned at all on top, and very smooth throughout. Serves 8.

## Mostaccioli with Sugo

1 pound mostaccioli or spaghetti, cooked according to package directions
3 medium-large red onions
1/2 carrot
1 garlic clove
1/4 teaspoon oregano
Salt and pepper to taste
2 pounds ground chuck
1 tablespoon parsley, chopped
Olive oil
1/2 to 1 cup Chianti or paisano wine
Catsup or Worcestershire sauce, optional

Finely chop onions, carrot and garlic (or grate in blender with a little olive oil). Stir onion mixture in heavy saucepan over medium heat until really brown. Set aside.

Brown ground chuck in Dutch oven, pouring off grease if necessary. Add parsley, oregano, salt and pepper. Add browned onion mixture to meat, mixing thoroughly. Add 1 tablespoon olive oil, then 1/2-cup wine, a little at a time. More wine or water may be added as meat simmers for an hour or so. Add dash of catsup or Worcestershire if desired. If sugo is too bland, try a little more pepper and/or wine.

Important: texture of meat sauce should be fine and grainy. Sugo serves best with mostaccioli. It can be made a day or two ahead of time; it improves with a little age. Serves 6.

## Tomato Sauce for Pasta

1/4 cup olive oil
1/4 cup butter
2 large onions, peeled and chopped coarsely
3 cloves garlic, minced
2 tablespoons minced parsley
  (or use 1 tablespoon dried)
1 teaspoon salt
Pepper to taste
2 green peppers, diced
1 large (1-pound, 12-ounce) can Italian plum tomatoes, broken up
3 tablespoons tomato paste

Heat oil and butter in heavy skillet or saucepan. Add onion and cook until lightly browned. Add garlic, parsley, salt and pepper. Cook, covered, over low heat for 15 minutes. Add green peppers and cook 5 minutes before adding the tomatoes. Simmer about 45 minutes, add tomato paste and stir over low heat until mixture is thickened and smooth. Taste and correct the seasonings. Serve over hot spaghetti or other pasta. Serves 3 or 4.

R. BRIGES

# Wedding Prelude

Here's a menu that, while perfectly suitable for any grand occasion, seems especially right for the dinner preceding the wedding rehearsal. Much of it can be done ahead of time, making things less hectic on the big day. Serve a cool white dinner wine with it, if you like.

### Charlotte's Pâté

1/2 pound chicken livers
1 tablespoon butter
1/4 pound butter
1/4 pound cream cheese
1 hard-boiled egg
1/2 cup sherry
1 10-ounce can clear consomme
1 envelope unflavored gelatin

Stir 1/4 cup of the sherry into consommé in a saucepan. Stir in gelatin and let mixture come to a boil until gelatin dissolves. Line an 8-inch glass pie pan with half of the consommé-sherry mixture. Place in refrigerator until firm. Meanwhile, brown chicken livers in the 1 tablespoon butter, add rest of the sherry, and let mixture cook 10 minutes. Put 1/4 pound butter, cream cheese and egg into blender with the cooked chicken livers and mix until all is creamy. Pour chicken-liver mixture onto consommé-lined pie plate, and smooth. Chill. Top pie with remaining consommé mixture. Place back in refrigerator until ready to unmold and serve. Best made the day before. 12 small servings.

### Lobster Thermidor

A dozen 8-ounce frozen lobster tails
6 tablespoons butter
1 cup sliced mushrooms
1 cup sherry
1/2 teaspoon salt
1 teaspoon paprika
1/4 cup flour
4 egg yolks
4 cups light cream
1 cup Parmesan cheese

Plunge frozen lobster tails into boiling, salted water and cook 11 minutes after water reboils. Drain and, when cool enough to handle, carefully remove meat from shells. With scissors or sharp knife, cut meat loose from the shell on the ends and edges. The meat can be pulled out then in one piece. Reserve shells.

Cut lobster meat in bite-sized pieces. Add meat and mushrooms to melted butter and simmer 5 minutes. Add sherry, salt and paprika. Cook 2 minutes. Sprinkle with flour and mix in. Beat the egg yolks with the cream and add

to hot mixture. Cook and stir gently until smooth and thickened. Spoon mixture into shells. Sprinkle cheese on top. At this point, they can be covered and refrigerated to finish in the oven the next day. Before serving, bake filled shells in a 350-degree oven 30 minutes (a little longer if they have been refrigerated) or until hot through and the cheese browns on top. Serves 12.

### Avocado Mousse with Grapefruit

2 tablespoons plain gelatin softened in
  1/4 cup cold water
2 small packages lime gelatin
4 cups hot water
2 cups sieved ripe avocado
  (5 or 6, depending on size)
1 cup mayonnaise
1 cup heavy cream, whipped
3 large grapefruits, sectioned, drained
Salad greens

Pour hot water over lime gelatin, stir, and add the softened plain gelatin. Stir until everything is thoroughly dissolved. Cool and refrigerate briefly, until thickened. Fold in all remaining ingredients. Pour into an 8-cup mold which has been greased with a little additional mayonnaise. It will set firm in 3 or 4 hours. May be made the day before serving. (After it jells, a little lemon juice rubbed on the surface helps keep the color.) At serving time, unmold onto chilled platter and garnish with salad greens and grapefruit sections. Serves 12.

### Spinach-Stuffed Pimientos

2 10-ounce packages frozen spinach
12 whole canned pimientos, drained
1/4 teaspoon nutmeg
1/2 teaspoon salt
1 teaspoon grated onion
3 tablespoons butter

Cook spinach according to package directions. Place drained pimientos in baking dish. Drain spinach well and chop. Add nutmeg, salt, onion and butter. Mix well and use to stuff the pimientos. Bake in a 350-degree oven for 20 minutes. 12 servings.

*Continued*

## Katherine Meringues

2 egg whites
1 1/2 cups sugar
6 tablespoons boiling water
1/4 teaspoon salt
1/2 teaspoon vanilla

In the top of a double boiler, mix all ingredients thoroughly and place over boiling water. Beat with rotary or electric beater at top speed until mixture stands in stiff peaks, but is not sugary. (This mixture is similar to the old standard "seafoam" or "seven-minute" frostings.)

Preheat oven to 225 degrees and cover a large cookie sheet with waxed paper. With a pastry bag or spoon, shape the mixture into 12 small meringues. (Recipe will make 36 tiny nibble-size puffs.) Bake 1 hour. The meringues should not brown. They will keep well in an airtight container for a couple of weeks.

*Filling:*

1 cup heavy cream, whipped
1/2 teaspoon vanilla
2 tablespoons sugar
1 10-ounce package frozen blueberries, thawed and drained (or substitute strawberries)
12 peach halves, canned or fresh, drained
For garnish: Maraschino cherries or candied violets

Flavor the whipped cream with vanilla and sugar. Reserve a little for topping, about 1/3 cup, then fold blueberries into remainder of the cream. Fill shells. Top each with peach half, a tiny dab of cream and garnish with cherries or violets. 12 dainty servings.

10

# A Bunch for Lunch

Entertaining the "girls"? Bridge? Shower? Club? The loveliest of luncheons is a savory baked sandwich, paired with an effervescent, fresh strawberry salad spiked with rosé wine, jellied and served in glass punch cups. Photographed at Locust Grove, the restored historic home of General George Rogers Clark in Jefferson County, Ky.

### Baked Ham and Cheese Sandwiches

    16 slices white bread, crusts trimmed
    8 slices ham
    8 slices turkey
    8 slices medium cheddar cheese
    6 eggs, beaten
    3 cups milk
    1/2 teaspoon onion salt
    1/2 teaspoon dry mustard

Make a single layer of 8 slices of bread in a greased baking dish. Top each slice with ham, turkey and cheese; then put the 8 remaining slices of bread over them. Mix remaining ingredients and pour over the sandwiches. Refrigerate overnight.

Top when ready to bake (1¼ hours before serving).

*Topping:*

    2 cups crushed cornflakes (this takes nearly a whole
      6-ounce box)
    1 stick (1/2 cup) melted butter or margarine

Mix well and distribute evenly over sandwiches. Bake 1 to 1¼ hours at 350 degrees. Slice into 8 portions. To serve, you may want to spoon a dab of hot, undiluted cream-of-mushroom soup over each portion. 8 servings.

### Rosé Strawberry Salad Mold

    1 6-ounce box strawberry gelatin
    1 1/2 cups boiling water
    1 1/2 cups rose wine
    1 quart fresh strawberries, hulled and sliced
      (sweetened if desired)
    1 8 1/2-ounce can crushed pineapple, not drained
    1 cup dairy sour cream

Dissolve gelatin in boiling water. Stir in rosé wine, strawberries and pineapple. Spoon half the mixture into punch cups (or large-size, paper cupcake-cups set in muffin rings; or individual fancy molds; or a large mold). Cups or molds should be about 1/3 full. Refrigerate until set. The remainder of the gelatin mixture should not be allowed to set, but should be syrupy.

Remove from refrigerator and spread sour cream over each mold. Now spoon remaining syrupy gelatin carefully over the cream. Refrigerate until set. Serve right in the punch cups. Or unmold, if you have used other molds.

You may want to garnish each serving with a bit of extra sour cream and a whole berry. About 10 servings.

The natural flavors here are wonderful. They really don't need sweetening, so use very little sugar if you do.

### Cocoa Muffins

    1 cup flour
    1/2 cup sugar
    1/4 cup cocoa
    2 teaspoons baking powder
    1 or 2 tablespoons butter or margarine
    About 2/3 cup milk

Sift the flour, sugar, cocoa and baking powder together. Using your fingers, rub the butter into the dry ingredients. Add enough milk to make a stiff batter. Spoon into greased muffin rings; 8 large ones or 14 tiny ones. Bake at 375 degrees 20 minutes for the large ones, 15 for the tiny ones. These aren't cupcakes; they're like old fashioned "sweetbread," flavored with chocolate. They're good dredged with powdered sugar. Or cut a cone from the top of each, fill with sweetened whipped cream, then replace the cone.

# A Cornish Repast

Sometimes a menu goes together with such grace that it keeps popping up again for special occasions. Case in point is this felicitous combination: Cornish hens roasted in herb butter, served on pistachio rice, with artichoke and mushrooms and curried fruit alongside. Dessert is a cream-filled nut roll, as delicate as it is memorable.

### Cornish Hens with Herb Butter

8 Rock Cornish hens, 12- to 16-ounce
1 lemon
1/2 cup butter, softened
1 1/2 teaspoons thyme
1 tablespoon salt

Wash and dry hens thoroughly. Salt the birds, inside and out. Cut lemon in 8 slices. Using 1 slice of lemon per hen, rub each bird inside and out. Then tuck the slice into the cavity. Mix thyme with butter. Put a lump of herb-butter inside each hen and dot rest of the butter on top. Tie legs together with string and place in open roasting pan. Bake at 325 degrees for 45 minutes to 1 hour, depending on the size of the hens, basting with pan juices 2 or 3 times during baking. It is well to have one 12-ounce hen for each diner. The 16-ounce bird may be split into 2 modest servings.

### Artichokes and Mushrooms

2 fifteen-ounce cans artichoke hearts, drained
2 one-pint packages fresh mushrooms
   (or 2 large cans)
4 tablespoons butter or margarine
1 1/2 teaspoons salt
1 tablespoon minced onion
2 tablespoons lemon juice
1 cup fine bread crumbs browned in 2
   tablespoons butter or margarine

Cook the mushrooms and onion in the ¼ cup butter until tender. In greased baking dish, arrange the mushrooms and artichoke hearts and sprinkle with salt. Drizzle the lemon juice over all. Brown the crumbs in a skillet with the 2 tablespoons of butter, stirring constantly. Sprinkle on top of the vegetables. Heat in 350-degree oven for 20 minutes. Serves 8.

### Curried Fruit

1 No. 2 1/2 can peach halves
1 cup dried apricots
1 small can pineapple chunks
1 1/2 cups brown sugar
2 to 3 teaspoons curry powder, according to taste
1/4 cup butter

Drain canned fruits. Soak apricots in juice for ½ hour or so. Then arrange all fruits in buttered baking dish. Cover with brown sugar. Dot the top with the butter and sprinkle with curry powder. Bake at 325 degrees for 45 minutes. This is a taste experience, very hot with the spice. "Sprinkle it on till you can smell it well." An ideal accompaniment for poultry of any kind. Makes 8 servings.

### Pistachio Rice

8 cups hot cooked rice, prepared according
   to package directions
2/3 cup shelled pistachio nuts, the amount
   you get from a 6-ounce package
1/3 cup melted butter or margarine (or
   substitute pan drippings from the roast
   birds for all or part of the butter)

When ready to serve, toss the rice with the remaining ingredients and put on a hot serving platter. Arrange the Cornish hens on the rice. Serves 8.

### Cream-Filled Nut Roll

5 eggs, separated
3/4 cup sugar
3 tablespoons fine dry bread crumbs
1 1/3 cup nutmeats finely grated or ground
1/2 teaspoon rum flavoring or 1 tablespoon rum
1/4 teaspoon salt

Beat the sugar and egg yolks together until very light. Beat egg whites with salt until they will hold stiff peaks. Stir the crumbs and nuts together, then fold the egg whites alternately with the nut mixture into the egg yolk-sugar. Add flavoring or rum. Turn into jelly roll pan, 15½-by-10 inches, which has been generously greased and lined with waxed paper. (Turn the waxed paper over on the greased pan to oil both sides of the paper.) Bake at 375 degrees for 20 minutes.

Carefully turn out on clean tea towel heavily sprinkled with powdered sugar. Starting with 1 long side, roll up, towel and all, and let cool. Gently unroll and fill with whipped-cream filling recipe below. Roll up again and chill thoroughly. Slice to serve. You may garnish with more cream and some pieces of whatever nuts you have used in the roll.

### Whipped Cream Filling

2 cups heavy cream, stiffly whipped
1 teaspoon vanilla
2 tablespoons powdered sugar

Fold the vanilla and sugar into the whipped cream. Fill the nut roll as described above. Makes 8 to 10 servings.

# Chow Mein, USA

For a money-saving meeting of East and West, try hamburger chow mein. And if ground beef seems a little out of character in this Oriental guise, just wait till you've tasted it! Make a spicy fruit mold for flavor contrast and end with a dessert light as spring air: Daffodil cake and serve it with lime sherbet topped with creme de menthe.

## Hamburger Chow Mein

3/4 pound hamburger or ground beef
1 small onion
1 can bean sprouts or Chinese vegetables
1 small can mushrooms
Vegetable oil or margarine
Soy sauce
Cornstarch and water
Chinese noodles or rice

Melt the margarine in a skillet or heat the oil, about 1 generous teaspoon. Add the onion and sauté until transparent and slightly yellow. Keep the heat low and let the transformation of the onion come about slowly.

Add the hamburger or ground beef. Break it up with a fork into small bits, and brown and braise until there is no pinkness left. Add bean sprouts or the Chinese vegetables along with the water in the can and thicken slightly with the mixture of cornstarch and water. Start with about 2 teaspoons of cornstarch mixed with enough cold water to form a thin paste, then add more if needed.

Let this mixture cook until it thickens some. Then add mushrooms—the canned stems and pieces can be used and the liquid from the can, too. Season slightly with salt and pepper, then add 2 tablespoons of soy sauce. Stir and heat, then taste; it may need more soy sauce or salt and pepper. Serve on the Chinese fried noodles or hot, fluffy rice. Serve with extra soy sauce handy.

## Spicy Salad Molds

1/2 cup English walnuts or California walnuts
1 envelope plain gelatin (1 tablespoon)
3/4 cup water
1/2 cup syrup from sweet pickles
2 tablespoons sugar
3 tablespoons lemon juice
1 cup undrained crushed pineapple
1 cup diced fresh or canned pears
Salad greens

Chop walnuts coarsely. Soften gelatin in 1/4 cup cold water. Heat the remaining water with pickle syrup, and dissolve the softened gelatin and sugar in it. Blend in lemon juice and pineapple. Cool until slightly thickened. Fold in pears and walnuts. Turn into individual molds and chill until firm. Makes 8 to 9 individual molds. Unmold on salad greens, or surround molds with salad greens.

Serve with mayonnaise or a French dressing.

## Daffodil Cake

### First Part

6 egg whites
1/4 teaspoon salt
1/2 teaspoon cream of tartar
3/4 cup sugar
1/2 cup cake flour
1/2 teaspoon vanilla

Beat the egg whites until frothy. Add salt and cream of tartar, and continue beating until stiff but not dry. Gradually beat in sugar, adding 2 or 3 tablespoons at a time. Gradually fold in flour, sifting it over the mixture or sprinkling it lightly over the top. Fold flour in gently but thoroughly. Add vanilla. Pour this mixture into an ungreased 9-inch tube pan.

### Second Part

6 egg yolks
1/2 cup sugar
2 tablespoons cold water
2/3 cup cake flour
3/4 teaspoon baking powder
1/2 teaspoon orange or lemon rind
1/2 teaspoon vanilla

Beat the egg yolks until thick and lemon colored. Add water, flavoring and sugar, and continue to beat.

Sift flour, measure and add baking powder. Sift again. Gradually add to egg mixture. Fold ingredients together until they are well blended.

Pour on top of the white batter and bake at 350 degrees for 1 hour. Invert as you would an angel-food cake to cool.

## Caramel Icing

1 cup tightly packed brown sugar
3 tablespoons shortening
2 tablespoons butter
1/4 cup milk
Confectioner's sugar

Mix ingredients and bring to a boil, stirring constantly. Let boil 2 minutes by the clock. Cool to lukewarm. Then add enough confectioner's sugar to make a consistency that will spread nicely, it takes about 2 cups. If you get it too stiff, add a little cream.

*Continued*

One of most sought-after recipes in Louisville in the 1940's, was the chicken chow mein served by the city's Brown Hotel. It's a lavish dinner in itself and all that's needed to top it off is a light chocolate-peppermint ice cream and some crispy oatmeal wafers.

## Chicken Chow Mein

2 hens (three pounds each, dressed)
1 pint fresh mushrooms, sliced
3 onions, sliced
3 celery stalks, sliced
1 No. 2 can bean sprouts
1 cup bamboo shoots, sliced
1 cup water chestnuts, sliced
10 cups chicken stock
1 1/2 cups cornstarch
1 1/2 cups soy sauce

Boil chickens, reserve stock. Cool chickens, cut them julienne style. Reserve one cup of shredded white meat on the side.

Fry mushrooms, onions, and celery in oil for a few minutes. Add stock and soy sauce and cook for a while, but stop while the vegetables are still crisp. Add bamboo shoots, water chestnuts, bean sprouts and chicken, bring to a boil and thicken with the cornstarch diluted with some stock. Season with salt and pepper.

Serve on fried Chinese noodles, allowing 1 No. 2 can for two persons. Top with a garnish made of the reserved julienne of chicken, 2 shredded leeks, a handful of chopped, toasted cashew nuts and 1 cupful of shredded pancake. (Recipe follows.) Mix the ingredients of the garnish up well and sprinkle on the chow mein.

The pancake mentioned above is made by mixing together 2 whole eggs, 2 tablespoons milk; 2 tablespoons flour. Mix well and pour into greased medium-hot skillet to make a very thin pancake. Turn to brown on both sides. Take from skillet and shred into thin strips. Serves 12.

## Chocolate-Peppermint Ice Cream

1 1/3 cups sweetened condensed milk
1 cup water
1/4 teaspoon salt
2 teaspoons vanilla extract
7 squares semisweet chocolate, melted
1 teaspoon mint flavoring
2 cups cream, whipped

Combine condensed milk, water, salt, vanilla, melted chocolate, and the mint flavoring. Mix well. Then fold in whipped cream. Put in freezer until half-frozen. Take out and beat with a spoon until smooth but not thawed. Return to freezing unit, cover with wax paper and freeze. Makes 8 servings.

## Oatmeal Wafers

2 cups sugar
3/4 cup butter or margarine
3 cups flour
3 cups rolled oats
1/8 teaspoon salt
1 teaspoon vanilla
1/2 teaspoon soda dissolved in 3/4 cup boiling water

Cream the butter or margarine with the sugar. Add vanilla. Add the rolled oats. Then add the flour (that has been sifted, measured and resifted with the salt) along with the soda and boiling water. Then fold in the rolled oats. Work on a lightly-floured board and roll out as thin as possible. Cut as desired.

Bake on ungreased baking sheet for about 10 minutes in a 400-degree oven. They should be lightly browned. Makes about 14 dozen cookies.

A. BRIGGS

# Oh, Do-Dah Day!

It's a menu like this, that calls into play Kentucky's distinctive harvest of delights, from leg of spring lamb and Bibb lettuce, to the homegrown ingredients for mint juleps, that sends Derby visitors away humming "My Old Kentucky Home."

### Mint Juleps en Masse

Make a simple syrup by boiling 2 cups sugar and 2 cups water for 5 minutes, without stirring. Fill a jar loosely with sprigs of fresh mint (uncrushed) and cover with the cooled syrup. Cap and refrigerate 12 to 24 hours. Discard mint. Make 1 julep at a time: Fill a chilled julep cup with finely crushed ice, pour in ½ tablespoon of the mint-flavored syrup and 2 ounces of the very best Kentucky bourbon. Frost, stick in a spring of mint and serve at once. You can get a head start by putting the first batch, without the mint sprigs, in the freezer. The refrigerator is not cold enough.

To frost: Grasp the rim of the filled julep cup with your fingertips and rapidly twist the cup back and forth until the outside is covered with a heavy frost. Or churn with a spoon.

### Rolled Cervelat

Put cream cheese through ricer, then add prepared horseradish to taste. Spread on thinly sliced cervelat (a smoked sausage) and roll. Stick toothpick in roll to hold together.

### Kentucky Spring Lamb Leg

A 7- or 8-pound leg of lamb
3/4 stick butter or margarine, softened
2 cloves garlic, minced
1 teaspoon salt
1 teaspoon paprika
1 teaspoon cayenne pepper

Place leg of lamb on a large sheet of heavy-duty foil. Mix butter with remaining ingredients and spread all over the lamb. Fold and seal the foil. Refrigerate overnight. Remove from refrigerator several hours before roasting time and allow it to come to room temperature. Don't remove the foil. Roast at 375 degrees for 35 minutes per pound. Serve with caper sauce. Serves 12.

*Caper sauce:*

1/2 bottle capers, drained and rinsed
1/2 cup heavy cream
1 can beef bouillon
2 tablespoons fat (use drippings from lamb roast)
1 tablespoon cornstarch

Blend cornstarch with lamb drippings in a saucepan, then gradually stir in the bouillon. Cook and stir until thickened. Add cream and capers, heat again until quite hot, without boiling. Serve in separate sauce boat, accompanying lamb.

### Watercress Dressing

1 cup watercress, large stems removed
1/2 cup parsley clusters
2 green onions, chopped
1 egg yolk
1 tablespoon tarragon vinegar
1/2 teaspoon Dijon-type mustard
1/2 teaspoon salt
Pinch of sugar
Cayenne
1/2 cup mayonnaise
1/2 cup sour cream

Put all ingredients, except mayonnaise and sour cream, in blender for 1 minute. Beat this mixture into the mayonnaise and sour cream.

Serve on cauliflower, tomatoes, or asparagus.

### Platter of Fruit in Wine Jelly

Use a silver platter with a well-and-tree and arrange the fruit on it artistically, building it up in the center. Keep the platter in the refrigerator and slide out the shelf for each coating, following directions for Gelatin Glaze. Select round fruits such as whole canned apricots, large strawberries, whole fresh black cherries, halves of peaches and pears, or preserved kumquats, being careful to place the rounded sides up. Half a peeled canteloupe makes a good foundation to build the fruit in the center. Tip pear and peach halves against its base and fill in with smaller fruit, using toothpicks to secure them if necessary. Small grape clusters are effective. Arrange the fruit in overlapping fashion from this beginning until the platter is covered, except for the well. If slices of banana, avocado, fresh peaches or pears are being used, be sure to dip them in lemon juice first. Chill the fruit arrangement before pouring on the first coating of gelatin.

Even though each fruit has been well drained, more juice will probably collect in the well. Dip this out first so as not to dilute the gelatin. A glass baster is helpful for this operation as well

*Continued*

Wes Kendall

as for glazing. Glaze with Wine Jelly. Dip up the jelly that runs into the well and return it to the liquid jelly. It will take about 10 minutes for each layer to congeal, and about 4 layers to encase the fruit properly. All this does not have to be accomplished rapidly—take your time. To serve, loosen the edges with a knife so that watercress may be tucked around it to form a crisp garland. Serve with Normandy Dressing.

*Wine Jelly:*

2 packages lemon-flavored gelatin
1 1/2 cups boiling water
1 1/4 cup cold water
1/4 cup lemon juice, strained
1 cup sherry

Dissolve gelatin in hot water, add other ingredients.

*Gelatin Glaze:*

Set jelly in a pan of ice water, stirring now and then so that it will chill evenly. Do not refrigerate or it will become lumpy. It is ready to use when it is the consistency of thick syrup. Keep a pan of warm water handy, as well as a pan of ice water, so the consistency can be easily controlled if the gelatin gets too thick or too thin. Whatever you glaze should be well chilled. Arrange on a serving platter and coat the whole arrangement, as in the platter of Fruit in Wine Jelly; or glaze its separate parts by placing a cake rack with a pan beneath to catch the drippings. It must be kept in the refrigerator to congeal between coatings. The easiest way is to slide the refrigerator shelf out each time and apply the gelatin without removing the dish. Put the amount you think you will need in a small pitcher and pour it over evenly or use a baster. (Use a soft brush in the final stages.) It will take about 10 minutes to congeal between coatings and it will take 4 or more coats. This is not at all difficult and will look most professional.

*Normandy Dressing:*

1 small package cream cheese, softened
2 tablespoons tart jelly
1 tablespoon lemon juice
Pinch of salt
3/4 cup heavy cream

Combine ingredients thoroughly, stirring in cream last. Makes about 1 cup.

## Asparagus Vinaigrette

Cooked asparagus (canned, fresh or frozen)
1/2 cup butter, margarine or salad oil
1/3 cup lemon juice or vinegar
1 teaspoon salt
1/4 teaspoon paprika
A good dash of fresh ground pepper
1 tablespoon chopped pimiento
1 tablespoon chopped cucumber pickle
1 tablespoon chopped green pepper
A grating of raw onion
1 tablespoon chopped parsley

In a small skillet or saucepan, melt butter or margarine. To this add lemon juice (or vinegar), salt, paprika and pepper.

Mix remaining ingredients together and add to the hot (but not cooked) butter and lemon juice. Swish in the skillet until hot but still not cooked. Pour over hot asparagus and top with grated egg yolk.

## Toasted Mushroom Loaf

1 loaf Vienna bread
1 pound mushrooms, sliced
2 sticks butter

Saute mushrooms in part of the butter, add the remainder and heat until melted. Cut Vienna bread in half lengthwise. Make deep gashes to form cubes about 1 1/2 inches square on cut side of both halves, cutting the bread crosswise and lengthwise almost to the crust. Spoon mushrooms and butter between the squares and over the top. Bake unwrapped, at 350 degrees for 20 minutes.

## Kentucky Sauce

1 cup brown sugar
1 cup white sugar
1 cup water
1 orange
1 lemon
1 cup bourbon
1 cup pecans, broken
1 cup strawberry preserves

Combine sugars with water and cook until syrup reaches about 240 degrees on candy thermometer, or until it will amost, but not quite, spin a thread. Remove from heat and stir in pecans and preserves.

Remove rind from orange and lemon with a potato parer and chop fine. Cut off and discard white membrane and remove sections. Cut orange and lemon sections into small pieces. Add cut-up rind, fruit, and the bourbon to the first mixture. Set away in refrigerator to ripen.

This recipe makes over a quart, but it keeps indefinitely. Serve it over ice cream.

# Tasty Antipasti

Antipasti, those glamorous and varied appetizers, can make or break a fine Italian dinner. Since they're so popular, why not play them up and lighten the rest of the meal? Add only wine-sauced veal scallopini on a bed of hot buttered noodles and a bit of fruit or sherbet.

## Chicken Giblet Pâté

3 cups chicken bouillon (use stock from boiling necks, wings and backs or make it by dissolving 3 bouillon cubes in boiling water)
3/4 pound chicken livers
1/4 pound chicken gizzards and hearts
1 bay leaf
A few celery tops
Salt, pepper and monosodium glutamate to taste
4 tablespoons butter
2 good-sized onions, sliced
1/4 cup chopped fresh parsley
1/4 teaspoon nutmeg
3 hard-cooked eggs, sieved
1/4 cup brandy or chicken stock
   for binding ingredients

Bring chicken bouillon to boiling. (If you have cooked bony chicken pieces, pick any meat from the bones and include it when you grind the pâté mixture.) Into boiling stock, place bay leaf, celery leaves, chicken gizzards and hearts. Add seasonings to taste and simmer until gizzards are tender, about 45 minutes. Remove giblets from liquid and cool. Melt butter in skillet and add the chicken livers and sliced onions. Cook, stirring occasionally, for 6 or 7 minutes. Don't overcook livers; they should be pink in the center. Remove and cool enough to handle.

Using the fine blade of meat grinder, grind together the cooked gizzards, hearts, livers and onion. The pâté should be very smooth, so it is a good idea to grind it twice. Place mixture in a mixing bowl and add parsley, sieved eggs and nutmeg. The most efficient mixer for this job is the human hand. Work the pâté, adding butter in which the liver was sautéed and enough brandy or stock to make a smooth spread, bearing in mind that it will be stiffer when refrigerated. Pack in small individual cups. Garnish with sieved hard-cooked egg, if desired, or decorate with mayonnaise piped on with a pastry tube. Six to 8 servings.

## Marinated Eggplant

1 small eggplant, not peeled, sliced 1/3 inch thick lengthwise
Salad oil to brush on eggplant slices
1/3 cup salad oil
1/4 cup vinegar
1 tablespoon honey
1 tablespoon chopped fresh parsley or 2 teaspoons dry
1 teaspoon chopped fresh mint or 1/2 teaspoon dry
Salt and pepper to taste

Brush sliced eggplant on both sides with oil. Place on cookie sheet and broil, turning once, until soft and slightly brown, about 5 minutes. Combine remaining ingredients to make a marinade. Layer eggplant with the marinade in a deep dish. Serve warm or cold as an appetizer. Four to 6 servings, depending on how many appetizers you are serving.

## Peppers with Anchovy Sauce

6 medium green peppers
2 cloves garlic, minced
6 anchovy fillets, plus oil from the can
1 tablespoon capers
Pepper to taste
1/4 cup wine vinegar
2 tablespoons salad oil

Place whole peppers on a baking sheet and place in preheated broiler. Broil, turning peppers frequently, until the skin blisters and loosens all over. This takes some watching, but the peppers are delicious when skinned. Cool and peel off skins. Cut into quarters and remove seeds. Combine garlic, anchovies, anchovy oil, capers, pepper, vinegar and salad oil, mashing the anchovies up with a fork. Mix and toss the dressing with the peppers. Serve cool. About 8 servings.

*Continued*

## Veal Scallopini

2 pounds round of veal, sliced 1/4 inch thick
Salt and pepper to taste
Flour to dredge meat
1/2 cup butter
1/2 pound fresh mushrooms, sliced, or equivalent canned mushrooms
1 large onion, chopped
1/4 teaspoon rosemary
1/4 teaspoon oregano
1 teaspoon parsley
1 cup dry white wine
1 teaspoon sugar

Have butcher slice veal thin. If you must do it yourself, it helps to partially freeze the meat. Salt and pepper the meat and dredge in flour. Melt half the butter (¼ cup) in skillet and brown the meat slowly on both sides. Remove to platter and keep warm. Sauté mushrooms in 2 tablespoons butter and set aside. Heat the remaining 2 tablespoons butter in skillet and sauté the onion with rosemary, parsley and oregano. Add mushrooms, wine and sugar. Taste and add salt and pepper if needed. Heat until very hot, but sauce should not boil after wine is added. Spoon sauce over veal and serve at once. Serves 6 to 8.

You may want to arrange hot, buttered, green or white noodles on the platter with the Scallopini. Drop 1 pound of noodles into a large pot of rapidly boiling, salted water. When tender, drain noodles and pour some hot water through them. Drain again and stir lots of butter in, ¼ cup or so. A half cup of fine dry bread crumbs may be added. Serve hot with Veal Scallopini. Six to 8 servings.

## Honeydew with Ham

1 honeydew melon, cut in thin wedges
1 1-pound package paper-thin slices ham

Simply wrap a slice of ham around each wedge of melon and add to your antipasto plate. This is a tasty substitute for the traditional, but expensive and hard-to-find, Italian ham, prosciutto.

## Stuffed Eggs

8 hard-cooked eggs
1 teaspoon dry mustard
1 teaspoon celery seed
1 tablespoon chopped pimiento
Salt and pepper to taste
Mayonnaise to bind

Shell and cut eggs in half, lengthwise. Remove the yokes, sieve them and add mustard, celery seed, pimiento, salt and pepper. Stir in enough mayonnaise to bind together. Pile into the hollows of the reserved egg whites.

# A Veal-Chop Meal

There is no nicer way to start a dinner than with soup. It's a fine beginning, especially when dinner will be tender, savory veal chops. Consommé that can be served jellied or hot is an excellent choice. Dieters will like it with a twist of lemon or lime. Others will enjoy a topping of curry-flavored whipped cream.

## Consommé

2 cans consommé
1 can water
1 can chicken broth
Freshly ground pepper
Curry powder
Toasted almonds
Extra gelatin, if you want it jellied

Mix the consommé, water and chicken broth together and simmer for 20 to 30 minutes, but don't boil. To serve the consommé jellied, soak 2 teaspoons plain gelatin in 2 tablespoons cold water and dissolve in the hot consommé. Chill until shakily jellied, then spoon into bouillon cups and serve with a slice of lemon or lime and whipped cream seasoned with curry powder to taste. Top off with a few toasted, slivered almonds.

## Savory Veal Chops

6 loin veal chops (with kidney, if you like)
2 tablespoons butter or margarine
1/4 teaspoon nutmeg
1 can chicken broth or soup
1 No. 1 can tomato juice (2 cups)
Pinch of savory
2 tablespoons chopped parsley
Pinch of cloves
3 peppercorns
Dash of white pepper
1 1/2 teaspoons salt
2 tablespoons flour
5 tablespoons cold water

Melt butter or margarine in a heavy skillet. Brown the chops. If your skillet cover is big enough, all the cooking may be done in the same utensil. If not, move the chops to a roaster. Dust the browned chops with nutmeg. Heat the chicken broth and tomato juice with 1/2 cup of water added and add 1 cup of the mixed liquids to the chops. Add the spices and seasonings. Blend and cook slowly over low heat for 10 to 12 minutes. Add the rest of the liquid. Cover.

Simmer slowly on top the range for about 45 minutes, turning the chops two or three times. Or, slide into a 325-degree oven for about the same length of time. The veal should be tender but not falling-to-pieces.

Remove the chops to a hot platter. Mix the flour with the 5 tablespoons cold water until smooth. Add to the juices in the skillet or roaster. Boil for about 3 minutes until the juices have thickened, and stir so the gravy will be smooth. Taste to judge seasoning.

Arrange chops attractively on the platter and pour some of the sauce over them. Serve the rest of the sauce in a bowl.

Fresh, sautéed mushrooms and toast cornucopias are easy and fun to add to the platter. Cut the crusts off thin-sliced bread. Roll lightly with a rolling pin. Then roll up in cornucopia shape. Fasten with toothpicks. Brush lightly with melted butter. Toast in a slow oven, about 350 degrees, until golden brown.

When the cornucopias have cooled some, take out the toothpicks. Serve stuffed with sprigs of parsley.

## Au Gratin O'Brien Potatoes

2 cups thinly sliced raw potatoes
1 quart boiling water
1 cup chopped onion
1 cup chopped green pepper
1/3 cup chopped pimiento
3 tablespoons melted butter
1/3 cup flour
2 cups warm milk
5 ounces (a cupful) grated American cheese
1 teaspoon salt
1/2 teaspoon pepper

Drop the thinly sliced raw potatoes into the quart of boiling water. Allow the water to re-

*Continued*

turn to boiling point. Add chopped onion and green pepper and let the water come to the boiling point again. Remove from heat and drain thoroughly. (Save the drainings to add to soup.) Add the chopped pimiento and mix gently.

In the top of a double boiler or heavy saucepan, blend the melted butter and flour. Add the warm milk, and cook and stir until the sauce is smooth. Add grated cheese, stirring until you have a smooth, thick sauce. Season with salt and pepper. Fold this sauce into the potato mixture.

Pour all into a 2-quart buttered casserole. Place casserole in a pan of hot water. Bake in a 350-degree oven for 1 1/2 hours, or until the potatoes are tender. Do not cover. Can also be cooked in individual casseroles. Serve 6 to 8.

## Pie Cake Pastry

*(Double the amounts for a 9-inch pie cake)*

    2 1/4 cups sifted enriched flour
    1 teaspoon salt
    3/4 cup shortening
    2 tablespoons sugar
    6 tablespoons water

Combine flour and salt in a mixing bowl. Use a pastry blender or two knives to cut in the shortening until the mixture looks like coarse corn meal. Sprinkle water over the mixture, one tablespoon at a time, and mix lightly with a fork until the flour is moistened. With the hands, gather dough into a ball and divide into smaller balls—it should make about seven. (Experiment for size on the first one.)

Roll 1/8-inch thick and cut to size with a 9-inch cake pan. Place on the turned-over bottoms of 9-inch layer pans. Prick well. Bake at 450 degrees for about 8 minutes.

Look in the oven after about 4 minutes, and if the pastry is forming blisters, prick again. The circles can be baked on cooky sheets, if it is more convenient, but baking them on the upside-down layer pans seemed to make better circles. Continue baking until you have the desired number of pastry rounds. Let cool.

To make the Pie Cake, put the pastry circles together with chocolate cream filling:

## Chocolate Cream Filling

*(Triple these amounts for the seven 9-inch layers.)*

    1 cup sugar
    1/3 cup water
    1/4 teaspoon cream of tartar
    3 egg yolks
    1/2 cup shortening
    4 ounces semisweet chocolate pieces
    1 teaspoon vanilla

Combine sugar, water and cream of tartar. Bring slowly to a boil and boil rapidly to 236 degrees on a candy thermometer, or until the syrup spins a light thread.

Beat the egg yolks until creamy and then, very gradually, beat in the hot syrup. Beat in the shortening, the melted semisweet chocolate pieces, and vanilla. Gently spread on one pastry round, and build upwards leaving the top of the last pastry plain except for a dusting of powdered sugar. Then garnish the pie cake with whole strawberries.

R. BRIGGS

# Teatime Tempters

"Tea quenches the thirst," goes an old Chinese saying.. "It gladdens and cheers the heart." Tea still has these effects, and you can suit it to your mood and the occasion. Whether it is to be a casual "Drop in for a cup" or a formal tea to honor a bride, serve beautiful food, too!

### Quiche Lorraine

A tea menu should include at least one delicious nonsweet—like this one—in addition to the usual cookies and cakes.

    1 9-inch unbaked pie shell
    1 1/2 cups coarsely grated Swiss or Gruyere cheese
    8 strips bacon, fried crisp and crumbled
    4 eggs, beaten
    2 cups thin cream, or "1/2 and 1/2"
    3/4 teaspoon salt
    1/4 teaspoon nutmeg
    1/4 teaspoon white pepper, or use black if you like

Place grated cheese in bottom of unbaked crust. Crumble bacon over cheese. Mix remaining ingredients and carefully pour over the bacon and cheese. Bake at 450 degrees for 10 minutes, reduce heat to 350 degrees and continue to bake for about 30 minutes, or until a knife inserted comes out clean. For teatime, cut in narrow wedges, serve hot or cold. Or it will make 6 supper servings.

### Four O'Clocks

*Cookie Dough*

    2 cups flour
    2 teaspoons baking powder
    3/4 teaspoon salt
    3/4 cup butter or margarine
    1 cup sugar
    1 egg
    1 1/4 teaspoon vanilla

*Brown-Eyed Cookies*

    2 tablespoons cocoa
    1/2 cup chopped nuts
    1/4 cup sugar
    1 slightly beaten egg white

*Cherry Ribbons*

    1/4 cup chopped maraschino cherries
    1/4 cup crushed, crisp cereal
    1/4 cup chopped nuts
    1/4 cup soft butter

Cream butter with the cup of sugar, add egg and vanilla. Beat well. Stir the flour, baking powder and salt together and add to the creamed mixture, mixing thoroughly.

To make the brown-eyed cookies, add the cocoa to 1/3 of the cookie dough, and form it into a square log an inch in diameter. Shape the remaining dough into a flat rectangle, four inches wide, and same length as the chocolate log. Place the chocolate log in the center of the plain dough and bring the edges up to enclose the chocolate.

Seal edges together, pat to square the form. Coat the log with egg white and roll in the nuts and sugar which have been combined. Chill several hours or freeze to facilitate slicing. Slice very thin and bake on lightly greased cookie sheets at 400 degrees, 8 to 10 minutes. Makes 4 to 5 dozen.

To make the cherry ribbons, chill, then pat out the basic dough into a rectangle about 1/3 inch thick and 6 inches wide. (Work with half the dough at a time; it's easier.) Mix the cherries, cereal, nuts and butter together thoroughly.

Spread some of the cherry mixture an inch wide along one long edge of the dough, then fold the dough to enclose it. Continue to spread and fold the dough, accordion style, until you have 3 ribbons of color encased in the dough.

Chill or freeze, then slice thin and bake on lightly greased cookie sheets at 400 degrees for 8 to 10 minutes. Makes 4 to 5 dozen.

With the basic dough, make half into ribbons and the other half into brown-eyed cookies for a pretty plateful!

### Asparagus Sandwiches

    12 tender cooked asparagus spears
    12 slices white bread, crusts off
    Soft butter or real mayonnaise

With a rolling pin, roll the bread slices flat. Spread with butter or mayonnaise. Roll up an asparagus spear in each slice, placing rolls close together so they won't unroll—or fasten with toothpicks—and chill.

Before serving, cut each roll in half. The half with the tip sticking out looks fine as is, but the blank half calls for the application of a thin olive slice for garnish. Makes 24.

*Continued*

## Cucumber Sandwiches

Thin slices of cucumber soaked an hour in salted
   ice water, drained
Circles of whole wheat bread
Softened butter stirred with a pinch of tarragon
   (optional, but good)

Spread the bread with herbed butter and
make sandwiches. Cover with foil or plastic
wrap and refrigerate until serving time.

## Yeast Snails and Fingers

For 2 coffee cakes or 4 dozen small rolls.

### Basic Sweet Dough

5 to 6 cups flour
2 packs or cakes of yeast
2/3 cup warm water (105 to 115 degrees)
1 cup warm milk (same temperature as water)
1/2 cup sugar
1 1/2 teaspoons salt
1/4 cup shortening or soft margarine
2 eggs, beaten

Sprinkle or crumble yeast into warm water
in a large, warm bowl and stir until dissolved.
Add warm milk, sugar, salt, shortening and eggs.
Beat in 3 cups of the flour, then add enough of
the remaining flour to make a soft dough which
doesn't cling to sides of the bowl. Turn out on
floured board or cloth and round into a ball.

Knead 5 to 10 minutes until dough becomes
smooth and elastic. Cover with a towel and let
rest 20 minutes. Punch down and divide into
halves. Shape into 2 coffee cakes or rolls as desired. (Topping recipes follow.) Place on greased
baking sheets. Brush surface of rolls with cooking oil and cover with plastic wrap.

Refrigerate 4 to 24 hours. (The cool-rise
method usually calls for refrigerating the
shaped dough 2 to 24 hours, but the longer mini-
mum of 4 hours is preferred.)

When ready to bake, remove from refrigerator and let stand for 10 minutes while oven
heats to 375 degrees. Bake small rolls about 20
minutes, or until done. Coffee cakes will take
25 to 30 minutes. Frost as desired.

### Cinnamon-Nut Topping

1/4 cup flour
1/4 cup sugar
2 tablespoons soft margarine
2 teaspoons cinnamon
1/2 cup chopped nuts

Combine ingredients. To shape "fingers,"
simply roll out half the dough into a rectangle
1/2 inch thick, spread with the cinnamon mixture and cut with a sharp knife into bars about
1/2 inch wide by 2 inches long. Place on
greased baking sheets and proceed with the
"cool-rise" refrigeration and baking instructions.

To shape snails, roll out the other half of the
dough, spread with the cinnamon-nut mixture
and roll up, sealing the loose edge securely.
Slice 1/2-inch thick and proceed as above.

### Lemon-Cheese Topping

1 8-ounce package cream cheese
1/4 cup sugar
1 egg yolk
1 tablespoon lemon juice
1/2 teaspoon grated lemon rind

Whip cream cheese, add sugar gradually. Stir
in remaining ingredients and beat until smooth.
Spread on coffee cakes or "finger" rolls after
brushing with oil and before the "cool-rise."
Or spread it on the dough for the "snails," roll
up and slice as outlined for the cinnamon rolls.

### Simple Glaze for Yeast Cakes

Combine 1 cup powdered sugar with 2 teaspoons milk or fruit juice. Spread on warm
cakes for thin glaze. It's thicker on cold cakes.

# Pig in a Smoke: Pork

A barbecued shoulder of pork, basted with a pungent sauce and served up with good, old-fashioned corn bread and turnip greens, plus some other tasty tidbits—this is a meal so rich in contrasting flavors it makes even the most jaded taste buds do nip-ups.

### Hickory Smoked Pork Roast with Virginia Smokehouse Sauce

4-to-5-pound pork shoulder, boned and rolled
1 tablespoon dry mustard
1 1/2 teaspoons cornstarch
3/4 cup beer
3 tablespoons lime or orange marmalade or tart jam
2 tablespoons molasses
1 clove garlic, put through press or very finely minced
1/4 teaspoon seasoned meat tenderizer
1 1/2 teaspoons liquid smoke

In a saucepan, combine dry mustard and cornstarch, adding just enough beer to work into a smooth paste. Add marmalade, molasses, garlic and seasoned tenderizer, blending thoroughly. Add remaining beer. Simmer until sauce is slightly thickened. Remove from heat and stir in liquid smoke. Makes about 1 cup.

Use oven rotisserie or portable spit—preheated to 325 degrees—or use any barbecue equipment with spit attachment. Secure roast on spit. Brush generously with the sauce. Barbecue 30-to 35-minutes per pound for an approximate total of 2 1/2-to 3-hours, basting frequently with the sauce.

If charcoal with hickory chips are added to the coals or briquettes, the timing must be adjusted to the heat of your coals.

Let finished roast rest about 20 minutes before carving, for more attractive and uniform slices. Make au jus gravy from the pan drippings. Simply skim off the fat and add water to thin. Serve very hot with the pork. Adjust seasonings. 4 to 6 servings.

### Sherried Raisins

Clusters of fancy raisins or regular raisins
Sherry

Heat some sherry—enough to cover. Place the raisins in a jar or bowl so it doesn't take too much sherry to cover them. Pour the sherry over the raisins and leave them to plump up.

### Turnip Greens with Turnips

Cut off turnip tops and pull the leaves down the stems, stripping them off. Wash, place in kettle with very little water. Bring to a boil, then turn the heat down and let the greens simmer. Season with butter, margarine or bacon drippings, salt and pepper, seasoning—salt and about 1/4-teaspoon monosodium glutamate. Turn leaves so all will be cooked evenly. Cook the leaves until tender.

There shouldn't be any liquid left in the kettle. If there is, raise the heat a little and allow it to evaporate. Taste to judge if more seasonings are necessary.

While the tops cook, peel the turnips and cut into quarters. Place in a saucepan, again with as little water as possible, and simmer-cook, after bringing to a boil in salted water, until tender. Don't overcook. Butter them, re-season with salt and coarse black pepper. Shake the saucepan to blend well.

When ready to serve, place the cooked turnip greens in the bottom of the bowl and the turnips on top.

Serve with lemon juice or with vinegar. If you like, use one of the flavored vinegars, such as basil or tarragon.

### Peanut Salad

1 1/2 cups shredded cabbage
1/2 cup diced apples
1 cup peanuts

Mix shredded cabbage and diced apples with peanuts. Serve with the following dressing:

*Dressing for Peanut Salad*

2 tablespoons sugar
2 tablespoons French mustard
1/2 cup distilled vinegar with 1/4 cup water
1/2 teaspoon salt
1 tablespoon cornstarch
1 egg
2 tablespoons butter
1/2 cup cream

Mix sugar, cornstarch and salt together. Add remaining ingredients. Cook until creamy. (A double boiler is best, stirring all the time.) Cool. When ready to serve, add another 1/2 cup sweet cream.

Toss the dressing lightly with the shredded cabbage and apples. Nestle the salad on a bed of green cabbage leaves and then strew a few more peanuts on the top.

*Continued*

## Skillet Bread

1 cup corn meal
1 teaspoon baking powder
1/4 teaspoon soda
1 teaspoon salt
1 or 2 eggs
3/4 cup sour milk or buttermilk
1/2 cup water
About 1 tablespoon shortening melted in hot iron skillet
  (9-inch) or bacon drippings

Sift together corn meal, baking powder, soda and salt. Beat egg, add to it milk and water. Add egg mixture to dry ingredients and mix well. Pour into hot skillet containing melted shortening or bacon drippings. Bake about 30 minutes in 400- to 450-degree oven. Invert on a plate and cut into pie-shaped slices. Serve skillet bread with plenty of butter.

## Frozen Lemon Pie

3 eggs, separated
Graham-cracker crumbs (about 1 cup)
Juice of 2 lemons (1/3 cup juice)
1 cup cream
1/2 cup sugar

Separate eggs. Beat yolks till light. Add 1/2 cup sugar. Beat in thoroughly and add juice of 2 lemons (the 1/3 cup) and also grated rind of 1 lemon. Whip cream and fold into the yolk mixture. Beat egg whites and then fold in. Line refrigerator pan with the graham-cracker crumbs. (Butter the sides and bottom of the pan then pat on the crumbs, saving a few crumbs for the topping.)

Pour in filling. Sprinkle crumbs on top. Freeze. Serve with ripe strawberries.

# Namesteak: Salisbury

There are days when one just doesn't feel up to dining upon filet mignon, but one must nevertheless eat! Salisbury steak, glazed with a savory brown mushroom sauce, is made with that old standby, ground beef, but it doesn't try to fool anyone. It doesn't need to, for it's a charming dinner on its own.

### Salisbury Steak

A pound of ground beef will make 3 large or 4 small servings.

For each pound of ground beef you will need:

1 egg
1/4 cup cream
1 slice bread, in fine crumbs
1/2 teaspoon Worcestershire sauce
1/2 teaspoon prepared mustard
1 teaspoon parsley flakes
1 teaspoon salt
1/2 teaspoon pepper
2 teaspoons cornstarch
A 4-ounce can mushrooms (stems and pieces)
1/2 cup beef bouillon or broth or 1/2 bouillon cube dissolved in a cup boiling water
For garnish: chopped fresh parsley

Combine meat, egg, cream, bread crumbs and seasonings. Form into patties and brown slowly in heavy skillet. (Sprinkle the frying pan with salt to keep it from sticking.) Remove to warm platter.

Mix the cornstarch with a little of the mushroom liquid. Pour off accumulated fat from the skillet and put in the mushrooms, liquid and all; the cornstarch mixture, and the beef bouillon. Stir and cook until transparent and slightly reduced in volume. Pour over steaks. Sprinkle with a drift of chopped fresh parsley, if desired.

### Rural Salad

4 large tomatoes
2 cucumbers
6 tablespoons crumbled feta or blue cheese
12 pitted ripe olives, halved
4 tablespoons vegetable oil
1/2 teaspoon basil
1/2 teaspoon salt
Dash of pepper (freshly ground preferred)

Peel tomatoes, if desired, and slice thinly. With tines of fork score cucumbers lengthwise and slice thinly. In shallow bowl arrange layers of tomatoes and cucumber; sprinkle with cheese and olives. Combine remaining ingredients; pour over all. Chill before serving. If a tangier dressing is desired, add 2 to 4 teaspoons lemon juice or wine vinegar to the oil, basil and pepper mixture. Makes 8 servings.

### Cheese-Broccoli Casserole

2 packages (10 ounces each) frozen, chopped broccoli
1 can cream of mushroom soup, undiluted
1/2 cup mayonnaise
1 tablespoon lemon juice
1/2 cup grated sharp cheese
1 jar (2 ounces) pimientos, chopped
1 cup crushed cheese crackers
1/4 cup slivered almonds or broken pecans

Cook broccoli according to package directions and drain. Arrange broccoli in a buttered casserole. Mix soup, mayonnaise, lemon juice and cheese. Spoon over broccoli. Top with pimientos, crackers and nuts. Bake at 350 degrees for 20 minutes. Makes 8 servings.

### "Pommes de Terre" Dessert

1 large (12-egg) angel food cake
1 cup powdered sugar
2 tablespoons cinnamon
Seven-minute frosting:
  1 1/2 cups sugar
  1 tablespoon white corn syrup
  3 tablespoons water
  1/2 teaspoon salt
  2 egg whites
  1 teaspoon vanilla
  1 cup finely chopped nuts

Cut the cake into 12 pieces, roughly rectangular. Blend the powdered sugar with the cinnamon in a bowl. Make the 7-minute frosting: In top of a double boiler, combine the sugar, corn syrup, water, salt and egg whites. Cook over boiling water, beating constantly, for 7 minutes, or until frosting stands in peaks. Add vanilla. Fold in nuts.

Coat each piece of cake with frosting, rather thinly, covering as much as possible while holding the piece. Then lay it, sticky side down, in the bowl of sugar-cinnamon. Finish coating the piece, then roll it well in the sugar mixture. It's quite easy to handle once it is in the sugar, and can be picked up and pressed into a shape closely resembling a potato. Makes 12 servings.

# Their Nibs: Ribs

Succulent, meaty spareribs are the nucleus for a hearty meal. In this menu, they're marinated in a sauce of soy and orange marmalade, then basted as they bake with the same mixture. They're great done on an outdoor grill, too. The dinner starts with freshly made cream of green pea soup, and ends with old-fashioned apple dumplings.

## Cream of Green Pea Soup

3 cups fresh or frozen peas
1 pint water
1/2 teaspoon sugar
1/2 cup chopped onion

Cook peas, adding sugar, in a saucepan until they are soft but still green. Force onion, peas and liquid through a food mill, or sieve, or put them in an electric blender.

Next make a cream sauce of:

3 tablespoons butter or margarine
3 tablespoons flour
1/2 teaspoon salt
1/8 teaspoon white pepper
3 cups milk

Melt butter in top of a double boiler. Add flour, salt and pepper. Cook over direct heat until the mixture is bubbly. Add milk; cook and stir over hot water until smooth. Combine the pea-mixture with white sauce and heat in a double boiler. Chopped chives or parsley may be added about 10 minutes before serving time. For extra flavor, add a dash of nutmeg.

## Mandarin Spareribs

4 or 5 pounds of meaty spareribs
1 cup soy sauce
1 cup orange marmalade
2 or 3 finely chopped cloves of garlic, or to taste
1 teaspoon ground ginger
A good-sized pinch of black pepper

Cut the ribs into serving-size pieces. Mix the soy sauce, orange marmalade, garlic, ground ginger and pepper together. Pour over the spareribs and let stand for 12 hours. Turn the ribs occasionally so the flavors of the marinade will penetrate the meat evenly.

Arrange the ribs on a rack in a roasting pan and roast them in moderate oven, 350 degrees, for approximately 1 1/2 hours or until tender, basting frequently with the marinade. The ribs should be glazed a beautiful brown color and the meat should be tender.

## Baked Hominy

2 cups cold cooked hominy, drained
1 cup milk
2 tablespoons butter, margarine or bacon drippings
2 eggs
1/2 teaspoon salt
1/4 tablespoon pepper

Heat milk and butter. Add hominy, and mix until smooth. Add beaten eggs and seasonings; then pour into a buttered baking dish. Bake at 350 degrees to 375 degrees until firm and brown on top—about 30 to 40 minutes.

## Apple Dumplings

### Crust Part

2 cups sifted flour
2 teaspoons double-acting baking powder or
    4 teaspoons single-acting baking powder
1 teaspoon salt
1/2 cup shortening
3/4 cup milk—or thereabouts

### Apple Part

6 small apples, pared and cored
1/2 cup sugar
1/4 teaspoon cinnamon
2 tablespoons butter or margarine

### Sauce Mixture

1/2 cup brown sugar, firmly packed in the cup
Dash of nutmeg
Dash of cinnamon
1/3 cup of butter or margarine
1 1/3 cups hot water

Sift flour and measure. Add baking powder and salt and sift into a bowl. Cut in shortening. Add milk and mix until you have a soft dough. Turn out on a lightly floured board and knead 30 seconds, or just enough to give it a smooth shape. Roll 1/8-inch thick and cut into squares, large enough to enclose a whole small apple, or if the apples are too large, core and pare and slice them up. Fill the core of each apple, or sprinkle the tops of the slices with some of the sugar and spices, plus butter listed in the apple part. Moisten the edges of the dough with cold water and bring the edges of the dough up over the apple or apple slices, pressing them together.

Place dumplings in greased pan, with plenty of room between. Prick pastry with fork. Combine brown sugar, nutmeg, cinnamon, butter and hot water of sauce mixture; heat until sugar dissolves. Pour sauce mixture over dumplings. Bake at 450 degrees 15 minutes; decrease temperature to 350 and bake 25 minutes more or until apples are tender. Serve warm with pan sauce and milk or cream.

# Kentucky Vittles

In 1952, Cissy Gregg selected recipes most typical of her home state, ranging from chicken fried in lard, to North Middletown beaten biscuits and Eastern Kentucky stack cake. The jam cake recipe included here became a classic—to this day, people ask for the recipe.

## Mrs. Creason's Jam Cake

5 eggs, beaten
2 cups sugar
3 cups flour
1 cup butter or shortening or part of both
1 cup buttermilk
1 teaspoon soda
1/4 teaspoon salt
1/2 teaspoon cinnamon
1 1/2 teaspoons cloves
1 1/2 teaspoons allspice
1 cup raisins or chopped dates
1 cup chopped nuts
1 cup jam—strawberry preferred—but any kind will do

Cream butter and gradually add the sugar. Cream together until light and fluffy. Add well-beaten eggs. Sift flour before measuring, and add to it the spices and the salt (the salt isn't necessary if you are using all butter).

Dissolve soda in buttermilk, and add it and the flour mixture alternately to the sugar-butter-egg mixture, beating after each addition.

Lightly dredge the nuts and fruit with a little extra flour, and add. Next add the jam. Stir to get good distribution.

Grease and paper-line two 9-inch cake pans, 2 inches deep. Bake at 325 degrees for 40 minutes, or until done. Ice with a caramel icing of your choice.

## Kentucky Rum Cake

1 cup butter
2 cups granulated sugar
3 1/2 cups flour, sifted once before measuring
3 1/2 teaspoons baking powder
1 cup milk, not too cold
8 egg whites, beaten stiff but not dry
1 teaspoon vanilla
Pinch of salt

Cream the butter and add the sugar a little at a time. Cream until fluffy. Add a third of the milk, flour and egg whites, in the order named, beating well after each addition, and beating well and long after the last addition.

Reserve 2 tablespoons of the flour, mix in the baking powder, and add this when all the beating is over, and the cake is going immediately into the oven.

At the very last, add vanilla and salt.

Bake in two 9-inch greased, paper-lined layer pans for 20 to 25 minutes, at 350 degrees. Turn out on racks and allow to cool before adding the filling.

**Filling:** Take 2 1/2 cups powdered sugar and 2/3 cup soft, creamed butter. Blend and beat until soft and smooth. (Sifting the powdered sugar makes the blending lighter work.) Add 4 ounces rum. Mix well again. Place in the refrigerator until the filling is firm enough to spread. The filling should be 1/2-to 3/4-inch thick.

After the filling is spread on the cake and the top layer placed in position, put filled cake in the refrigerator until the filling is set and the frosting is ready.

**Frosting:** Use 2 cups granulated sugar and enough water to moisten the sugar well. Boil together until the syrup will spin a thread. Pour slowly in a fine stream over 2 beaten egg whites. While the mixture is hot, add 12 marshmallows, a few at a time, and then add 1 or 2 teaspoons of rum. Pile high on the top and spread the sides smoothly.

## Fried Chicken

Choose young chickens that weigh approximately 2 1/4 pounds when dressed. Disjoint into serving pieces—the Kentucky way is two or three pieces of breast, legs, thighs, wings, upper and lower back.

Melt 1 pound of lard in a large, heavy, deep skillet on the order of a Dutch oven. Heat the fat very hot.

In the meantime, dredge the pieces of chicken with seasoned flour—flour, salt, pepper and paprika. Coat the pieces with all they will take.

Drop the pieces of chicken into the hot fat. When they're a golden brown, reduce the heat some and allow them to cook through. The meatier pieces take from 25 to 30 minutes, but the backs and wings will cook more quickly.

There should be enough fat actually to deep-fry the chicken.

Drain on absorbent paper and serve on a hot platter. Chicken cooked this way is wonderful cold, too.

*Continued*

Fried Chicken

Beaten Biscuits

Mrs. Creason's Jam Cake

## Beaten Biscuits

7 cups flour
1 cup lard
1 teaspoon salt
2 to 4 tablespoons sugar
1 teaspoon baking powder
1 1/3 cups cold milk

Sift the flour and measure. Then sift flour, baking powder, salt and sugar together three times.

Cut in the lard, using the fingertips, or two knives, or a blender. Work until the shortening and flour are of a consistency finer than for regular biscuits, but not as fine as for pastry.

Add the cold milk to make a stiff dough.

If using a "bread break," get the dough into a ball, flatten it out, turn the crank, and start running it through the machine. A bread break looks like a clothes-wringer.

Fold and run it through again. Keep doing this until the dough is slick, glossy, and the large blisters that air forms in the dough pop.

Roll 1/4-inch thick and cut with a biscuit cutter—use a 2-inch one. Then make three rows of impressions with the tines of a fork which pierce the biscuit through to the bottom.

If the dough is beaten by hand, beat out until about 1/4-inch thick. Fold and beat again. Repeat this until the dough is smooth, glossy and has blisters. Finally roll the dough out as given above, cut and mark with a fork. Do not add any more flour in either method of handling.

By hand, it takes 30 minutes to beat biscuits. You can do them in 15 minutes on a machine.

Bake at 350 degrees for 20 to 25 minutes, or a little longer. If the biscuits are to be served straight from the oven, they should be only a delicate brown. If they are to be reheated, bake them completely, but leave the final browning until the reheating process.

## Massie Stack Cake

3/4 cup shortening
1 cup sugar
1 cup sorghum molasses
3 eggs
1 cup milk
4 cups flour
1/2 teaspoon soda
2 teaspoons baking powder
1 teaspoon salt
3 cups evaporated applesauce, or old-fashioned dried apples cooked to make a thick filling. Season apples with spices to taste

Mix thoroughly flour, salt, soda and baking powder by sifting together three times. Cream shortening, then add sugar, a little at a time, blending well.

Add sorghum and mix thoroughly. Add eggs one at a time, beating after each addition. To this, add flour and milk alternately, and beat until smooth.

Place mixture, 3/8-inch thick, in floured 9-inch cake pans. Bake at 375 degrees for 18 minutes. This should make six layers.

When cool, stack up layers, using applesauce generously between each layer.

Applesauce seasoned with cinnamon, cloves and nutmeg, cooked down thick, goes through the batter layer and the combination is delicious. It should stand to "cure" before cutting.

**Massie Stack Cake**

38

# Chinese Oodles

Just one of the beauties of Chinese cuisine is the small size of nearly everything; no knives appear in the place settings. And, since there's rice, there's no need for bread. The variety is astonishing; a traditional meal includes fish, pork, fowl, beef and eggs. These authentic recipes are from a dinner party of a group of Louisville's Chinese residents.

## Sub Gum Shrimp

1 pound fresh shrimp, cleaned and split in half
1 cup young pea pods, cut in halves or 1/2 cup fresh
   or frozen green peas
1/2 cup bamboo shoots (canned), sliced
1 teaspoon salt
2 tablespoons sherry wine
Dash of pepper
1 1/2 teaspoons cornstarch
1/2 teaspoon sugar
3 tablespoons vegetable oil
2 slices fresh ginger or 1/8 teaspoon ground ginger
1 tablespoon water
1 scallion, cut in 1/2-inch lengths

Combine one teaspoon of the cornstarch, 1/2 teaspoon of the salt, the pepper and the sugar and dust over the prepared shrimp; drizzle with the sherry. Meanwhile, heat 1½ tablespoons of the oil in a skillet over medium-high heat until hot. Add the shrimp which has been coated with the spices and sherry; the ginger and the scallion, then sauté, stirring gently for about three minutes.

Wash skillet, or use another, and heat remaining 1½ tablespoons oil until hot. Add pea pods (or peas), bamboo shoots and the remaining salt. Stir-fry (or sauté) about one minute. Add a mixture of the water and remaining ½ teaspoon cornstarch and stir-fry for two more minutes. Then add the previously cooked shrimp and stir gently until heated through.

## Chow Bok Toy

1 pound (about two stalks) Chinese celery cabbage
   washed and cut into one-inch diagonal strips
1 teaspoon soy sauce
1/2 teaspoon monosodium glutamate
1 teaspoon sugar
1/2 teaspoon ground ginger
1 teaspoon sherry wine
1/2 cup water
1 1/2 tablespoons vegetable oil
1 tablespoon salt

Mix the seasonings (except salt) with the water and wine and set aside. Put oil in a skillet

and heat; add salt. Then put white or stalk portion of the Chinese celery cabbage in the skillet and stir-fry two minutes. Add the green leafy portion and stir-fry another minute.

Add the previously prepared mixture. Stir and cook for one more minute and then cover and cook two more minutes.

For variety, bits of country ham or pork may be added.

## Fahn Keh Ngow Yook

1 tablespoon peanut or vegetable oil
1/4 teaspoon salt
1 clove garlic, crushed (optional)
1/2 pound flank or sirloin steak, sliced very thin
   (about 1/8 inch)
1 cup onion, sliced thin
1 cup fresh tomatoes, cut diagonally
1 cup green peppers, cut diagonally
1 fresh scallion (white part only), slivered
1 teaspoon monosodium glutamate
1 1/2 teaspoon soy sauce
1/2 teaspoon sugar
Dash of black pepper
2 tablespoons sherry wine
1/2 teaspoon ginger, preferably fresh-shredded
1/4 cup bouillon
1 tablespoon cornstarch

Put oil in hot skillet, add salt and garlic. Stir-fry one minute; add the steak and stir-fry another minute; add tomatoes, peppers and onions and stir-fry one more minute. Add the scallion and stir-fry another 1 1/2 minutes. Then mix together monosodium glutamate, soy sauce, sugar, pepper, wine and ginger; add and stir-fry one minute more. Add bouillon; cook just until it comes to a boil. Do not cover!

Meanwhile, mix the cornstarch with enough water to make a thin paste. Add and stir constantly until the gravy thickens. It should be served over rice.

## Gai Yick

Remove the tips from chicken wings (thrifty cooks will make soup from these) and make a slit in the skin between the bones of the re-

*Continued*

maining pieces. Into the slit stuff little bundles of strips of country ham, green onion, canned bamboo shoots, and if you can find them, Chinese mushrooms. (The mushrooms should be presoaked about an hour, or until soft, in lukewarm water.)

Place the stuffed chicken wings on a heat-resistant plate (a pie plate will do) on a rack in a large pan which has a small amount of water in the bottom. Cover and steam very slowly for about 2¾ hours. Remove chicken wings, thicken the drippings with cornstarch and pour gravy over the wings. Arrange on platter and serve piping hot.

### Yerng Doong Goo

Soak dried Chinese mushrooms in lukewarm water until softened, about an hour. Remove stems, turn the caps upside down, and stuff with chopped or ground pork loin to which have been added diced, canned water chestnuts and very finely diced green onions. Season the "stuffing" with salt and a little soy sauce.

Place stuffed mushrooms on heat-resistant plate set on a rack in a frying pan, with a small quantity of water in the bottom, and steam slowly for about an hour.

### Hai Foo Young

1/2 cup crabmeat
1/2 cup onion, chopped fine
1/2 cup scallions, chopped fine
1/2 cup bean sprouts
1 teaspoon seasoning powder
1/2 teaspoon salt
1/4 teaspoon pepper
4 eggs, beaten
1/4 cup mushrooms, chopped
1/4 cup celery, chopped fine
1/4 teaspoon garlic powder

Pour about ½-inch peanut or vegetable oil into a frying pan and heat to medium hot.

Mix all ingredients together throughly; divide into three or four portions, and fry (like an omelet) in the hot oil until golden brown on both sides.

Drain on paper towel.

This is a basic Foo Young dish but any kind of meat, fish, or chicken may be substituted for the crabmeat. Lobster, shrimp, roast pork, ham, veal and beef are all good.

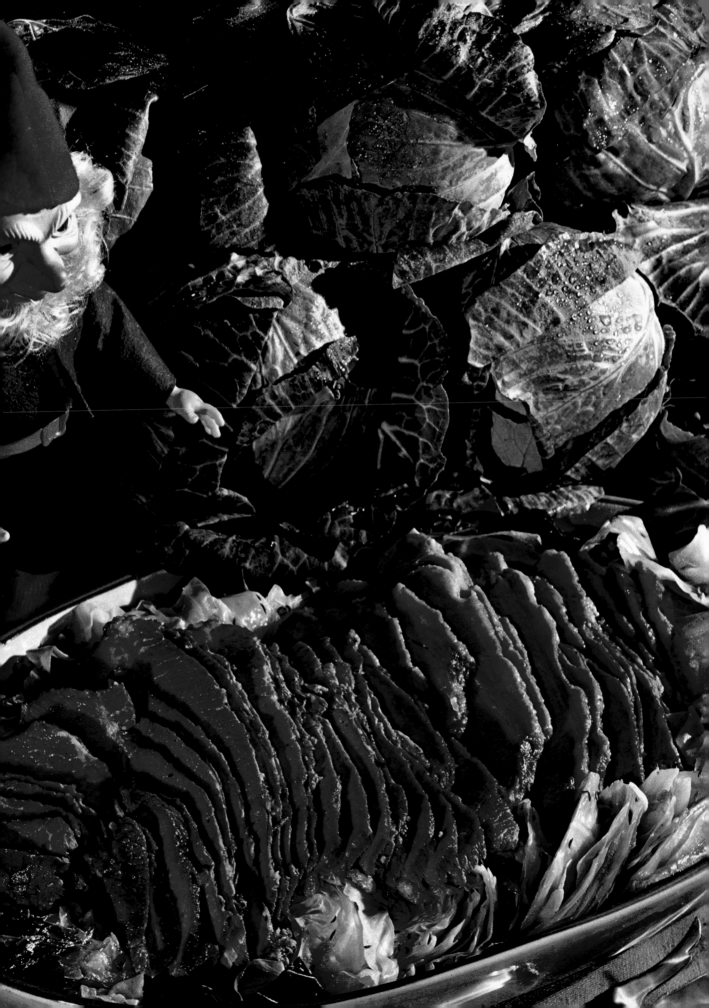

# Pot Luck o' the Irish

If you learned about Irish food from the comic strip, "Bringing up Father," then you know that corned beef and cabbage, with some potatoes on the side, constitute the backbone of the Irish diet. So, especially for St. Patrick's Day, corned beef and cabbage it must be, with a salad that carries a touch of the green, and an Irish Trifle for dessert.

## Corned Beef and Cabbage

A 4- to 5-pound piece of corned beef
1 teaspoon whole cloves
6 or 8 whole peppercorns
1 bay leaf
1 stalk celery, broken up
A large head cabbage, cut into wedges or slices
1/2 teaspoon caraway seeds

Place beef in a large kettle and pour cold water over to cover. Add cloves, peppercorns, bay leaf and celery. (If the corned beef came in a plastic pack, loaded with flavoring materials, you may want to cut down on the spices called for here.) Bring to a boil, cover and simmer 4 to 5 hours, or until tender. Skim the foam away a few times during the cooking.

When meat is tender, remove from liquid and keep it warm. Strain the broth and return it to the kettle. Bring to a boil and drop in the cabbage. Add caraway seeds and simmer about 20 minutes, or until it is tender. Lift cabbage from broth with a slotted spoon and arrange it on a warm platter. Slice corned beef very thin and place on cabbage. Serves 8 to 10.

## New Potatoes

Many people cook small new potatoes along with the cabbage. Just scrub them and leave their pink jackets on. But cooked separately, lightly-salted and buttered, they seem to retain more of their distinctive flavor. Either way, they are the perfect accompaniment for corned beef and cabbage.

## Donegal Salad

2/3 cup raw spinach
1 3/4 cups mayonnaise (not salad dressing)
3 hard-cooked egg yolks
Lettuce
Celery hearts
3 hard-cooked egg whites, sieved

Place spinach, broken up, into electric blend-er with mayonnaise and egg yolks. Run motor until mixture is smooth and pale green throughout. Place 2 or 3 small stalks of trimmed celery on lettuce for each individual salad and fill cavities with the green mayonnaise. Sprinkle tops of each salad with the sieved egg white. Serves 8.

## Irish Trifle

A stale bakery sponge cake, round or loaf,
   7- or 8-inch size
1/2 cup raspberry jam
1/3 cup Irish whiskey
2/3 cup sherry
Custard (recipe below)
Topping (recipe below)

With a sharp knife, split the stale cake into 4 layers. Spread each layer with jam, then re-stack the cake in a glass dish with sides. Mix Irish whiskey with sherry and pour over cake. Cover with a plate and let stand an hour or more.

*To make custard:*

1 egg plus 2 yolks
2 tablespoons sugar
2 cups milk, scalded

Beat the egg, yolks and sugar together in the top of double boiler. Slowly beat in the scalded milk. Stir and cook over hot (not boiling) water until it thickens. Pour, while hot, over the cake. Let stand until cold.

*To make topping:*

2 egg whites
1 cup heavy cream
1 tablespoon sugar
For garnish: 1/3 cup toasted almonds

Beat the 2 egg whites. Whip the cream and blend in the tablespoon sugar. Then fold the beaten egg whites into the whipped cream. Pile over the trifle. Decorate with spikes of toasted almonds. Serves 8.

# Grill-Watcher Menus

In parts of the country where winter makes itself felt, it can seem a long time between cookouts. Here are Barbecued Beefburgers to open the season, then, as well as the absolute best in accompaniments: Colorado Baked Beans, Bacon 'n' Egg Potato Salad and Strawberry Ice Box Cake.

## Barbecued Beefburgers

3 pounds ground chuck
3/4 cup quick-cooking oatmeal
3/4 cup milk
2 teaspoons salt
1 tablespoon horseradish

Mix ingredients thoroughly and shape into patties. Grill to desired degree of doneness, basting frequently with sauce.

This recipe will give you about 12, thick, juicy beefburgers that fit 5-inch sesame seed buns.

### Barbecue Sauce

1 small onion, chopped fine
3/4 cup catsup
1/4 cup vinegar
1/4 cup water
1 teaspoon hickory-smoked salt
1/2 teaspoon chili powder
1 tablespoon Worcestershire sauce
1/4 cup brown sugar

Mix ingredients and boil 20 minutes. Strain. Brush on burgers as they grill. These are delicious when done in the oven, too. Just prepare the patties and arrange them in a flat baking pan. Overlapping won't hurt. Stir up the barbecue sauce and, without boiling or straining it, pour on half and bake at 325 degrees for about an hour, basting with more sauce as necessary to keep the patties looking juicy. They'll be done at the same time as the baked beans, and still taste like a cookout.

## Colorado Beans

1/2 pound salt pork, cubed, or 8 slices bacon
4 large onions
1/2 cup brown sugar
1/2 cup vinegar
1 can green lima beans
1 can white lima beans
1 can "pork and beans"
1 can kidney beans

Fry salt pork or bacon until done. Remove from skillet and cook onions until transparent. Add sugar and vinegar. Drain all beans except "pork and beans" and add to onion mixture, along with salt pork or crumbled bacon. Bake in 2-quart casserole or bean pot at 325 degrees for 1 hour. 12 servings.

## Bacon 'n' Egg Potato Salad

About 8 good-sized potatoes, boiled, peeled, sliced
1/2 cup bottled French dressing
1 teaspoon pepper
1 large onion, chopped
8 slices bacon, fried crisp and crumbled
1 cup mayonnaise, more or less
1 tablespoon salt
1 tablespoon celery seed
4 eggs, hard boiled and thinly sliced
1/2 cup sliced, stuffed olives

Mix the French dressing and salt with the warm sliced potatoes and let stand while you ready the rest of the ingredients. Sprinkle on the pepper, celery seed, chopped onion, egg, bacon, olives. Add mayonnaise last and mix gently. Taste and correct seasonings. Serves 12.

## Anchovy-Caper Cream

1 cup mayonnaise
1 cup sour cream
2 tablespoons anchovy paste
2 tablespoons capers, chopped

Mix; chill. A dip for raw vegetable chunks.

## Icebox Cake

3 pints fresh strawberries (Save 12 nice ones for garnish; slice the rest)—or raspberries, or fresh peaches
1 1/2 cups heavy cream, whipped
3/4 cup very soft butter
1 egg plus 1 egg yolk, beaten
2 cups vanilla wafer crumbs (Reserve 2 tablespoons for topping)
1 1/2 teaspoons vanilla (Put 1/2 teaspoon of this in cream when whipped)
3 cups powdered sugar (Put 2 tablespoons of this in cream when whipped)

Cream butter and sugar, add beaten egg and 1 teaspoon vanilla. Consistency should be pourable but not watery. If mixture seems too thick, set the bowl in a pan of warm water and stir till thin enough to pour. Now put half the wafer crumbs on bottom of a 9-inch spring form pan or other pan of about 2-quart capacity.

Pour half the creamed mixture over the crumb layer. Add half the berries next, then half the whipped cream. Repeat layers. Sprinkle reserved crumbs on top. This dessert should be partially frozen. Put in the freezer for one hour before serving or, if made ahead, keep frozen until about an hour before serving. Garnish each portion with a whole berry. 12 servings.

*Continued*

For your next cookout, try leg of lamb this way and you'll never want to eat anything ordinary again! Bone the leg, flatten it, marinate it and grill it lovingly to perfection over charcoal. Serve with Tabooley Salad, a delightfully astringent parsley and mint combination from the Middle East.

## Grilled Butterfly Leg of Lamb

A leg of lamb, about 6 pounds
3 garlic cloves, minced
1 teaspoon salt
1/2 teaspoon dried mint
1/2 teaspoon "lemon pepper" or ordinary pepper
1 teaspoon marjoram
2 tablespoons grated onion
1/2 cup salad oil
1/2 cup lemon juice

Have your butcher bone and flatten the leg of lamb; it will spread like a thick steak, and take on a sort of "butterfly" shape.

Combine remaining ingredients to make a marinade. A plastic bag the right size to fit the meat makes the best container for the job, as you don't need to turn the meat. Or use a flat enamel or glass pan. Marinate the meat at least 2 hours at room temperature, turning frequently, or marinate in the refrigerator overnight, making sure meat is well covered with mixture. At cooking time, drain off the marinade.

To keep meat flat while cooking, use a grill basket if you have one. If not, insert 2 long skewers to form an X through the meat. Grill over medium coals 1 1/2 to 2 hours, turning and basting every 15 minutes, till medium to well done. Most prefer meat to be somewhat pink in the center. To carve, remove skewers and slice thin, against the grain. Should serve 10 to 12.

For a delightful improvement, try 3 or 4 leaves of fresh mint, put through a garlic press, instead of using dried mint.

## Calico Baked Beans

1 can (1 pound) butter beans
1 can (1 pound) red kidney beans
1 can (1 pound) vegetarian beans in tomato sauce
2 tablespoons butter
1/2 cup chopped onion
1/2 cup chopped green pepper
1 1/2 cups shredded American cheese
1/2 teaspoon salt
2 large tomatoes, sliced
More cheese, sliced

Drain butter beans and kidney beans thoroughly and combine with vegetarian beans in a buttered 1 1/2-quart casserole. Melt butter in skillet, add onion and green pepper and sauté until onion is transparent.

Combine onion, green pepper, shredded cheese and salt with beans. Bake at 350 degrees for 30 minutes. Remove from oven and top with tomato and cheese slices. Return casserole to oven and bake about 10 minutes, or until very hot and lightly browned. Serves 8.

## Tabooley Salad

1/2 cup cracked wheat, soaked several hours in cold water
2 large bunches fresh parsley
1/2 cup chopped fresh mint
1 cup chopped green onions, tops and all
4 or 5 large ripe tomatoes, cubed small
Juice of 4 lemons
1/2 cup olive oil
Salt and pepper

Wash the parsley carefully, remove stems and chop coarsely. Add the mint, onions, tomatoes and the soaked cracked wheat which has been drained in a sieve. (When you drain it, press all possible moisture from it.) At serving time, add lemon juice, olive oil and the salt and pepper. A nice touch is to line your salad bowl with fresh grape leaves. This salad is one of the most perfect complements to serve with lamb.

Cracked wheat just about doubles in volume when soaked in water. These broken whole wheat grains are available in stores, but sometimes are very difficult to find.

## Herbed French Bread

One long loaf French bread
1 stick butter or margarine, softened
1/2 teaspoon oregano
1/4 teaspoon thyme
1 teaspoon poppy seeds

Slice loaf in 1-inch slices, down to but not through crust. Mix butter with oregano, thyme and poppy seeds and spread mixture on every cut surface. Wrap loosely in foil. At serving time, bake 12 to 15 minutes at 400 degrees or until hot. Serves 8.

# Middle-East Eating

A staple in the Middle-Eastern diet for many centuries, laban has lately been discovered by everybody else to be a "health food." You may know it as yogurt, and it is only the beginning when the St. Michael's Eastern Orthodox Church of Louisville stages its annual "smorgasbord."

## Green Beans with Lamb

1 pound lamb, cubed
2 tablespoons butter
2 pounds green beans
1 onion, minced
1 No. 2 can tomatoes (minced)
Salt and pepper to taste
1/4 teaspoon cinnamon
1 cup hot water

Cook beans until tender, drain and set aside. Brown the lamb and onion in butter, add the cup of hot water and simmer 10 minutes. Add beans, tomatoes and seasonings. Simmer 30 minutes to combine flavors or finish cooking in oven at 325 degrees.

## Stuffed Cabbage Leaves with Spice

1 head new tender cabbbage (2 pounds)
1 pound small diced lamb shoulder or breast
  (beef may be substituted)
1 cup long-grain rice, soaked 10 minutes
1/2 teaspoon cinnamon
1 tablespoon salt
1 tablespoon pepper
1/2 teaspoon allspice
1/8 teaspoon cloves
1 No. 2 can tomatoes, mashed, or
  2 cups tomato juice
1/4 cup lemon juice
1/4 cup melted butter

Remove core from cabbage and immerse in boiling water for 5 minutes, until leaves will separate without breaking. Separate leaves and cut off part of the coarse rib so leaf will roll easily. Mix meat and rice. Add spices and melted butter. Put about 2 tablespoons meat mixture in each leaf and roll, closing the ends by folding them inside, then fastening with wooden picks.

Line Dutch oven with a couple of outer cabbage leaves, then lay the rolls on them evenly. Add 2 cups water and cook, covered, on low heat for 20 minutes. Add tomatoes and lemon juice and cook slowly either on top of stove or in 325-degree oven for 40 to 45 minutes or until tender. Uncover and cook 5 more minutes. Serves 4 to 6.

## Stuffed Grape Leaves

1 cup long-grain rice, soaked 10 minutes
A few rib bones of lamb
1 pound lamb, diced fine
2 tablespoons melted butter
1/4 teaspoon cinnamon
1 teaspoon allspice
1 tablespoon salt
1/2 teaspoon pepper
1/4 cup lemon juice
20 to 30 grape leaves (buy brined ones in jars or use
  fresh ones, making sure they are young and tender)

Line bottom of cooking vessel such as Dutch oven with bones and a few grape leaves. Mix drained rice with lamb, butter and seasonings. Roll about a tablespoon or more of meat mixture in each grape leaf, turning in corners and fastening with wooden picks. (Put filling on the back of leaf.)

Place rolls evenly in pan and add water to come about 1/4 inch above leaves. Weight the stuffed leaves with a plate, cover pan and simmer about 30 minutes. Add lemon juice and simmer an additonal 5 minutes.

## Laban (Yogurt)

1 quart milk
1/4 cup laban culture (or use commmercial yogurt;
  instructions follow)
2 tablespoons warm milk

Mix laban culture with the 2 tablespoons warm milk until smooth. Cover and set aside. Heat the quart of milk in a saucepan just to boiling point, remove from fire and pour into a heatproof bowl or porcelain casserole. Cool about 8 minutes, or to 110 degrees on a candy thermometer.

Add laban mixture to milk, stir well and put in a warm place to set. It will take 4 to 5 hours. The custom is to wrap the bowl in a towel. An unlighted oven is a good place to put it, if the house is air conditioned. Refrigerate and use as needed.

To use commercial yogurt as a starter, first bring the milk to 180 degrees, then cool to 110

*Continued*

degrees before adding 1/2 cup yogurt. Be sure to save 1/2 cup each time for future culture.

Use laban as a dressing for sliced cucumbers, garnished with mint. Or mix it with puréed fruit, equal parts, for a fruit-flavored yogurt. Try freezing it in cubes as "suckers" for children.

## Ratatouille

1/2 pound zucchini, sliced crosswise 1/2-inch thick
1 medium eggplant (about 1/2 pound) pared and cut like large French fries
1/2 cup olive oil
1/2 pound onions, sliced
1 cup sliced green pepper
2 cloves garlic, minced
1 pound ripe tomatoes or 1 cup pear-shaped tomatoes, drained
Salt and pepper to taste
3 tablespoons minced parsley
2 teaspoons basil

Place the sliced zucchini and eggplant in a large mixing bowl and sprinkle with a teaspoon salt. Let stand 30 minutes. Drain on paper towels. Heat a little olive oil in large skillet and saute the zucchini and eggplant, one layer at a time, removing to another container as they cook. Add oil as needed and put in green pepper and onions.

Peel tomatoes, cut crosswise and gently squeeze seeds out. Cut them coarsely and add to peppers and onions in skillet. Cook slowly, shaking pan occasionally, or stirring gently for 15 minutes. Return eggplant and zucchini to pan. Add parsley, basil, salt and pepper and simmer, covered, for 5 minutes. Uncover, stir gently and cook until most of the liquid has evaporated and vegetables are tender. Serves 6.

If you prefer, place the cooked vegetables in a casserole in layers and bake at 350 degrees, basting with natural juices, for about ½ hour.

## Chicken Stew

2 2-pound frying chickens, quartered or cut in serving pieces
2 tablespoons butter
4 medium onions, quartered
2 cups (or a No. 2 can) tomatoes
2 large potatoes, cubed
Cinnamon, salt, pepper, to taste

Simmer the chicken in a little water for 20 minutes. Melt the butter in a separate pan and cook the onion in it just until wilted. Add to chicken, along with the tomatoes, and continue cooking slowly for another 20 minutes. Then add potatoes and seasonings and cook for another 20 to 30 minutes, or until chicken is tender. Serve the chicken stew over hot rice. Recipe will make 6 to 8 servings.

## Turkish Delight

8 envelopes gelatin
2 cups sugar
1 cup water
1/8 teaspoon salt
1/2 cup undiluted frozen orange juice concentrate
1 cup finely chopped nuts

Blend gelatin, sugar and water in 3-quart saucepan. Add salt, place over low heat and stir until all is dissolved. Simmer 20 minutes, stirring occasionally. Remove from heat; add orange juice. Chill, stirring occasionally, until slightly thickened. Stir in nuts. Rinse an 8-inch square pan with cold water, pour in mixture and chill until firm. Unmold on board or cloth dusted with confectioners' sugar. Cut into small squares. Roll in more sugar. 1 1/2 pounds.

R. BRIGGS

# Let's Croquette

Next time you roast a chicken, don't eat it; hoard it to make these croquettes! These are the only croquettes known that are even more delicious than the original chicken they were designed to use up! And serve broccoli, of course, but with character. Plus a heavenly grapefruit aspic with a secret ingredient nobody can guess.

## Nanny's Chicken Croquettes

4- to 5-pound hen
1/4 pound butter
2 tablespoons flour
2 cups single cream
Salt and pepper to taste
1 can cream of mushroom soup
1 cup chopped mushrooms
Bread crumbs
3 or 4 eggs

Cook hen until tender. Let cool, then chop coarsely. Melt the butter, add flour and blend together well. Add the cream and cook until thick. Season to taste. Add the mushroom soup. While still hot add the cut up chicken and chopped mushrooms and stir well. Set in refrigerator overnight.

Next morning drop by tablespoon onto wax paper covered with bread crumbs. Shape into logs three inches by one and one half inches. Roll well in crumbs. Beat three or four eggs until well mixed. Dip croquettes in egg and roll in crumbs again quickly, so as not to lose egg. Store in refrigerator until ready to use. Drop in deep hot oil (375 degrees) and fry until brown. Makes about 2 dozen croquettes.

## Grapefruit Aspic Salad

1 3-ounce package lemon gelatin
3/4 cup boiling water
1/2 package plain gelatin
1 tablespoon cold water
1 cup grapefruit juice
2 cups grapefruit sections
1/4 teaspoon salt
1 tablespoon sugar
1 teaspoon (or more) grated onion
1/2 cup slivered almonds (optional)

Dissolve lemon gelatin in the boiling water. Add the soaked plain gelatin, grapefruit juice, salt, sugar and grated onion. (The onion flavor no one can guess.) Let the mixture set until syrupy. Add grapefruit sections (they may be cut in half) and the slivered almonds. Spoon into 6-cup mold. Serves 8.

## Broccoli With Celery Sauce

2 packages frozen broccoli
1 can cream of celery soup
1 can water chestnuts

Cook broccoli according to package directions. Drain. Heat cream of celery soup, undiluted. Add thinly sliced water chestnuts. Serve hot over broccoli. Serves 8.

# Great Outdoors!

A party served outdoors, whether on a patio or just a grassy spot made comfortable with seating for all, gives a nice dimension to entertaining. This spaghetti dinner scaled for a couple of dozen people, takes on a more festive air from being served out where there's a balmy breeze.

## Celery Stuffing

Combine equal parts of softened butter and peanut butter. Season highly with salt, cayenne and add a few chopped pimiento-stuffed olives.

## Marinated Olives

1/2 cup of olive oil (salad oil can be used, but all or part olive oil is preferred)
2 slices lemon
1 clove garlic, peeled and quartered (use 2, if small, or more flavor is desired)
Olives

Put olive oil in a jar which has tight-fitting lid. Add the lemon and garlic. Drain liquid from the olives and dry olives on a cloth. Add them to the jar of seasoned oil, put on jar lid and turn upside down a few times so the olives will be well-coated with the oil. Set in refrigerator overnight· Pricking the olives with a fork will help them absorb more flavor.

## Bologna Pie with Chives

2 packages cream cheese
Cream or top milk to moisten
1/4 cup chopped chives
1 pound sliced broad bologna

Mash the cream cheese with a fork. Moisten with sufficient cream to make a smooth paste. Fold in the chopped chives and mix until well blended.

Carefully remove the casings from the bologna so the slices won't tear. Place the first slice on a plate and spread generously with the filling. Place another slice on top and spread again. Continue until you have a stack the height that can be handled on a toothpick. Leave the top slice unspread. Wrap and set in refrigerator until thoroughly cold. Slice into wedges and stick toothpicks in the wedges for easy handling.

## Artichoke Hearts in Olive Oil

24 small canned artichokes
1/2 cup lemon juice
3 cups dry white wine
2 tablespoons wine vinegar
3 bay leaves
3 cloves
6 peppercorns
1/4 lemon, cut in thin slices
Also: olive oil; 3 more bay leaves; 4 more peppercorns

Drain artichokes and pour the lemon juice over them. Mix together wine, vinegar, bay leaves, cloves, the 6 peppercorns and lemon slices. Simmer together for 10 minutes. Pour over the small artichokes. Put in the refrigerator to set overnight. Next day, drain thoroughly and place in a large jar. Cover with olive oil, bay leaves and peppercorns and let stand in the jar for 3 days. Add more oil if the artichokes absorb it so that it doesn't cover. Store in a cool place and they will keep a long time.

## Italian Spaghetti Sauce for 25

2 pounds ground beef
1 pound ground pork
3 green peppers
2 pounds onions
1 pound mushrooms, sliced
3 cans Italian tomato paste
3 cans water
3 No. 2 cans tomatoes
1 small red-hot pepper
3/4 cup salad oil
Salt
3 pounds spaghetti
1/4 pound grated Parmesan cheese
2 cloves garlic, minced

Sauté onions, garlic and green pepper in oil for 20 minutes. Add meat and break it into small pieces as it cooks. Cook the meats with onion, garlic and green pepper for 1/2 hour. Add tomato paste diluted with the cans of water, and the tomatoes. Add red pepper broken into small pieces, and the salt. Simmer 1 to 2 hours until the sauce has thickened. Stir occasionally to keep the sauce from sticking.

Boil the spaghetti 10 minutes in salted water.

*Continued*

Drain. Pour boiling water over it. Mix sauce and spaghetti or serve spaghetti, sauce, and cheese separately, mixing each serving.

Always put spaghetti in a hot dish or on a hot platter and have the serving plates warmed.

## French Dressing

1/2 teaspoon salt
1 clove garlic rubbed on a cube of bread
1/3 teaspoon anise
5 tablespoons tarragon vinegar
1 teaspoon beau monde
1 teaspoon sugar
Dash of thyme
3 pinches of dry mustard
1/4 teaspoon fresh ground pepper
Cayenne pepper
Dash of Worcestershire sauce
Dash of Maggi sauce

Combine all of these and let stand for 15 minutes. Then add 1/2 cup salad oil and 1 cup peanut oil. Shake vigorously. Add 1 tablespoon chopped parsley and 1 tablespoon sherry.

## Crisp Bread Sticks

1 cake yeast
1/4 cup lukewarm water
1 cup warm milk
1/4 cup butter
3 cups sifted flour
1/2 teaspoon salt
1 tablespoon sugar

Dissolve yeast in water. Dissolve butter in milk. Sift dry ingredients. Combine liquids. Add flour. Knead lightly. Let rise until double in bulk. Knead again, adding enough flour to handle. Let rise again. Knead until smooth. Cut into pieces the size of walnuts. Roll into sticks 10 inches long and the width of a lead pencil.

Place 1 inch apart on greased cookie sheet. Let rise again until they are twice the size. Bake in a 425-degree oven 5 minutes then at 325 degrees until crisp.

## Fruit Compote

Sweeten fresh fruits to taste with powdered or confectioners' sugar. If you use canned fruits, the syrup from them is your sweetening agent. Add lemon juice to taste, or use a tablespoon of sherry wine for each serving. Blend well with the fruit and place in refrigerator for at least 2 hours to mellow. Stir a couple of times during this period, gently, so the fruit or berries won't be broken up. There should be enough juice on the fruit to serve as a "sauce" with the fruit.

## Sand Tarts

3/4 pound butter, soft but not melted
1 1/2 cups granulated sugar
3 eggs
1 1/2 cups flour

Cream sugar and butter. Add salt to butter, if it is unsalted. Stir in unbeaten eggs. Add enough flour to make a soft dough. They must be rolled very thin: Use a cover on the rolling pin, chill the dough, and roll part of it at a time. If the dough seems a little soft after chilling, add a little more flour. Shake flour lightly over board and rolling pin. Roll out dough, cut in any shape and place on a greased tin. Brush milk over each cookie. Sprinkle with mixed cinnamon and sugar and place a small pecan on each. Bake in a 400-degree oven for a few minutes.

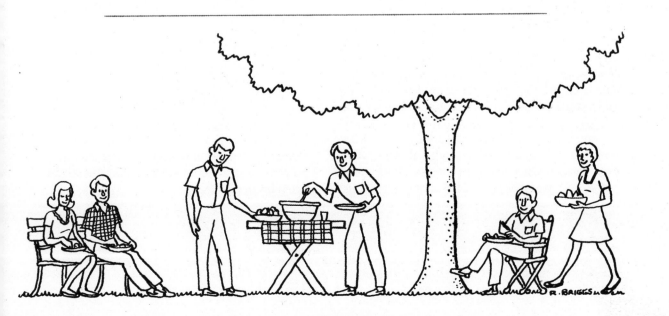

# Gourmet Grilling

If outdoor cookery is your forte, you'll want to add Saki Flank Steak to your repertoire. Do the marinating in a plastic bag so you don't have to keep turning it over and over. After the grilling is done, slice the meat paper-thin, diagonally. The flavor is like no other.

### Saki Flank Steak

1 1/2 pounds flank steak, not scored
1/4 cup soy sauce
1/4 cup saki (or substitute sherry)
1/4 cup salad oil
2 teaspoons powdered ginger
1 clove garlic, crushed
1 teaspoon sugar

Make marinade by combining all the ingredients except the steak. Then place the steak in the marinade and allow to marinate for 24 to 48 hours. Drain well. Grill over hot charcoal 4 to 5 minutes. Slice very, very thin, on the diagonal. Serves 3 to 4. Steak fixed this way is great cold for hors d'oeuvres.

### "Real Man-Type" Potatoes

4 or 5 good-sized potatoes, sliced thin
1/2 green pepper, chopped
1/2 onion, chopped
Salt and pepper to taste
Butter or margarine

Arrange sliced potatoes in layers on a large piece of heavy-duty foil and sprinkle each layer with salt and pepper. Top each layer with chopped pepper and onion and dot with butter. Fold foil securely and place on grill close to coals. Turn once after 15 minutes. They should be done in about 1/2 hour, if the layers aren't stacked too thickly. Makes 6 servings. You may wrap potatoes in 6 individual foil packets. Variation: Cover each layer with cheese slices; omit onion and green pepper. Grill without turning.

### Salad on the Spot

Firm, fresh vegetables (celery, carrots, cucumbers, lettuce, radishes), a cupful per person, cut into large "bites"
Salt and pepper to taste
1/2 pound or more sharp cheddar, cut into 1-inch cubes and halved
Small jar stuffed olives
1 cup mayonnaise
1 clove garlic, split, impaled on toothpick

Place washed vegetables in heavy plastic bag and refrigerate until last possible moment. Take along the cheese in a separate plastic bag. Place garlic in mayonnaise and carry in covered plastic dish. At serving time, just roll down the top of the bag of vgetables, sprinkle with salt and pepper. Toss in the cheese bites and the olives, well drained. Remove garlic from mayonnaise. Let each person serve himself, using the garlic mayonnaise for dunking the bites.

### Potato Chip Cookies

1 cup butter
1/2 cup sugar
1 egg yolk
1 teaspoon vanilla
1 1/2 cups flour
1/2 cup crushed potato chips
1/2 cup chopped nuts

Cream the butter and sugar. Add rest of ingredients. Drop by teaspoonfuls on an ungreased cookie sheet. Bake 15 minutes in a 350-degree oven. Cool slightly, and then roll the cookies in powdered sugar.

# For Salad Days

A glorious salad needs and deserves to be served in a bowl that's clean and fresh. Since a buildup of stale oil and garlic gives the wooden salad bowl an air not in keeping with the freshness that gives a salad distinction, wash and dry it quickly after each use. And fill it repeatedly with one of these classic salads!

### Green Goddess Salad

1 large head iceberg lettuce
1 clove garlic, cut in half
8 anchovy fillets and 1 tablespoon oil, or 2 tablespoons anchovy paste
1 cup mayonnaise
2 tablespoons tarragon vinegar
1/4 cup chopped chives
1/4 cup chopped parsley
2 scallions or green onions, chopped fine
1/2 teaspoon tarragon

Core lettuce, wash in cold water and drain. Wrap and refrigerate. Mash anchovies with oil (or use anchovy paste) and blend in mayonnaise, vinegar, chives, parsley, scallions and tarragon. Let dressing stand for an hour to develop flavor. Tear up lettuce into bowl, add dressing and toss lightly until each bit is well-coated. 6 large servings.

### Caesar Salad

1 large head iceberg lettuce
1 clove garlic, crushed
3/4 cup oil, preferably olive
2 cups day-old bread cubes
Freshly ground black pepper to taste
2 eggs
1/4 cup lemon juice
1/2 cup grated Parmesan cheese

Core lettuce, wash in cold water and drain well. Place in plastic wrap and refrigerate. Add garlic to oil and let stand several hours or overnight.

Heat ¼ cup of the garlic oil in skillet and sauté bread cubes in it, stirring frequently, until browned on all sides. Drain on absorbent paper.

Tear up lettuce into salad bowl; sprinkle with salt and pepper. Add remaining ½ cup garlic oil and toss until every bit of lettuce is coated. Break eggs into center of lettuce, add lemon juice and toss until well mixed and creamy. Add Parmesan cheese and croutons, toss lightly and serve immediately: 6 large servings.

### Crab Louis Salad

1 package (10-ounce) frozen cut green beans
1 1/4 cups mayonnaise
1 teaspoon seasoned salt
1/2 teaspoon salt
1/8 teaspoon pepper
3 tablespoons chili sauce
1 large head iceberg lettuce
2 cans (6 3/4 ounce) crabmeat, drained and flaked
1 cup carrot slices, crisp-cooked
2 medium tomatoes, peeled and sliced
2 hard-cooked eggs, sliced

Cook green beans according to package directions, drain and chill· Blend mayonnaise with seasoned salt, salt, pepper and chili sauce to make a Thousand Island dressing. Core lettuce and arrange leaves in salad bowl. Arrange crabmeat, carrots, green beans and tomato slices on lettuce. Garnish with sliced eggs and serve with the dressing. 8 servings.

### Guacamole Salad

1 medium-head iceberg lettuce
1 ripe avocado
2 tablespoons lemon juice
1/2 cup mayonnaise
1 small onion, chopped
1 small can green chili, chopped
1/2 teaspoon salt
Dash Tabasco
2 large ripe tomatoes, peeled and sliced

Core lettuce, wash, drain and refrigerate. Peel and pit avocado and mash it smooth. Blend in lemon juice, mayonnaise, onion, chili, salt and Tabasco. Shred lettuce and arrange on platter. Top with tomato slices. Heap gaucamole over tomatoes. Makes 8 servings.

# Cook In, Eat Out

There are days when the best course is to pack up a picnic and head for the nearest park, leaving all cares behind. Chicken, as it is fried at Boone Tavern in Berea, Ky., is the main thing to take along. For sandwiches, make the best pimiento cheese ever. And you'll be glad you made so many crispy oatmeal cookies.

### Berea Fried Chicken

1 fryer, cut in serving pieces
1/2 cup pancake mix
Salt and pepper
1 egg, beaten
2 tablespoons milk
Deep fat for frying

Steam chicken for 20 minutes. This can be accomplished by placing chicken in a sieve over boiling water. Cover and allow to steam.

Mix salt and pepper into pancake mix.

Beat egg and milk together.

Dip chicken in egg mixture, then roll in pancake mix until pieces are well coated.

Heat fat and fry chicken until golden brown.

### Pimiento Cheese Sandwiches

2/3 pound mild cheddar cheese
1 4-ounce jar pimiento
3 medium-sized sweet pickles
1 teaspoon sugar
1/2 teaspoon salt
1/4 teaspoon pepper
1/2 cup or more mayonnaise

Grind the cheese, pickles and pimiento. Mix in the sugar, salt and pepper. Add enough mayonnaise to make the mixture spreadable. The sandwiches may be assembled and frozen the night before, then taken from the freezer when you pack your picnic in the morning. By noon they will have thawed nicely, and lettuce can be added. They're very good if taken right from the freezer and grilled, too!

### Salad on a Stick

These are the same vegetables usually taken along on picnics, but presented a little differently. Cut the vegetables into good-sized bites and impale them on a wood or metal skewer, at the rate of one well-furnished skewer per person. Wrap each serving in plastic wrap to transport.

### Egg Soup

Egg soup is quite easy to make and take in a vacuum bottle to a picnic. While you're frying the chicken, put the bony pieces you don't use with a few extra backs if you have them, into a kettle with 5 or 6 cups of water, and simmer gently for an hour. (If the broth doesn't seem rich enough, after it has been strained from the bones, add a bouillon cube or two and a bit of butter.)

1 quart boiling chicken broth
1/3 cup flour
1/2 teaspoon salt
1 egg yolk

Combine flour, salt and egg until mixture is in crumbs. Rub through the hands into the bubbling broth. Take hot soup to the picnic in a vacuum bottle and serve it in paper "hot cups."

### Crisp Oatmeal Cookies

2 cups shortening
2 cups sugar
2 1/2 cups brown sugar, firmly packed
4 eggs
5 teaspoons soda, dissolved in 1/2 cup water
5 1/2 cups flour
5 1/2 cups quick-cooking oatmeal
1 teaspoon salt
2 teaspoons vanilla
3 cups (15-ounce box) raisins, optional

In large mixer bowl, cream sugars with the shortening. Add eggs, one at a time, while beating. Add water mixed with soda, the salt and vanilla. Still in the mixer, blend in about half the flour, stopping when the mixer begins to feel overworked. Transfer mixture to a huge bowl and mix in the rest of the flour and the oatmeal. The best possible tool for stirring up such a quantity is the human hand. If you use raisins, work them in last. Form into 5 or 6 rolls, 1 1/2 to 2 inches in diameter, depending upon how large you like them. Freezing for a couple of hours makes them easy to slice for baking. Slice 5 or 6 cookies to the inch and bake at 375 degrees for 10 or 12 minutes, on ungreased baking sheets. These cookies will keep indefinitely in the freezer. The recipe will make 12 to 15 dozen.

# Stew? Veal Ragoût!

It isn't often that veal is to be found in the butcher's display case. But when you do find it, you'll need this tasty ragoût recipe. Of course ragoût is a stew, but when it is as elegant as this one, with mushrooms and almonds, it must be called ragoût. Slow simmering is the secret; cooking temperature should be between 150 and 170 degrees.

## Veal Ragoût

2 pounds veal (cut in 1-inch cubes)
3 tablespoons flour
1 teaspoon salt
1/2 teaspoon paprika
2 medium onions, chopped
1 clove garlic
2 tablespoons olive oil
1 cup tomatoes
1 carrot, sliced
2 1/2 cups hot water
1/2 teaspoon curry powder
Salt
Pepper
2 tablespoons wine, or use vinegar, or lemon juice
1/4 pound mushrooms (dice the stems
   and slice the caps)
1/2 cup salted almonds

Take the cubes of veal and roll them in flour which has been seasoned with salt, pepper and paprika. Sauté meat, onions, and garlic in olive oil until well browned. Add tomatoes, carrots, water, seasonings. Cook covered until the meat is tender. Add wine, mushrooms and almonds, and cook uncovered until mushrooms are tender—about 5 minutes. Serve with rice or noodles and a tossed green salad.

## Creamed Spinach

In a skillet, put 2 tablespoons bacon drippings. Add enough flour—about one full tablespoon—to thicken the drippings slightly. Cook until blended, stirring constantly. Have cleaned, cooked, chopped spinach ready. Add it to the bacon drippings with a little water, some grated onion, and a small handful of grated bread crumbs. Then add salt and pepper. Steam; add the white of 1 egg, then stir rapidly and constantly. Serve immediately.

## Strawberry Cream

2 eggs, separated
1/2 cup sugar
Pinch of salt
1 tablespoon lemon juice
1 envelope unflavored gelatin
1/4 cup cold water
1 pint strawberries, washed, hulled, and crushed
1 cup cream for whipping

Beat egg yolks in top of double boiler until thick and lemon-colored. Then blend in sugar, lemon juice and salt. Cook, stirring constantly, over simmering water about 5 minutes, or until sugar dissolves and mixture is smooth and custard-like; remove from heat. Soften gelatin in could water in large bowl; pour in hot egg mixture; stir until gelatin is dissolved. Blend in strawberries; chill until syrupy. Beat egg whites in small bowl until stiff but not dry. Lightly fold into chilled strawberry mixture. Beat cream until stiff in same small bowl; fold into strawberry mixture. Spoon into 1 1/2-quart mold; chill 2 to 4 hours, or until firm. Serve plain or garnish with whole strawberries. **Makes about 8 servings.**

# Leftover Ham: Right!

Here's a lovely dinner built around the last pound-and-a-half of a baked ham. If the ham has been a large one, by this time its welcome has begun to wear thin. So grind it up and pour on the seasonings. Presto! It's a whole new thing.

## Ham Loaf

1 1/2 pounds cooked lean pork, ground
1 1/2 pounds cooked ham, ground
1 can (10 1/2 ounces) tomato soup
1 1/2 cups milk
2 eggs
1 cup cracker crumbs
1/4 cup finely chopped onion—more or less
1/4 cup chopped green pepper
1 1/2 teaspoons monosodium glutamate
1/2 teaspoon salt
1/4 teaspoon pepper

Grind the pork and ham together. Mix all ingredients lightly but thoroughly. Pack the mixture into a lightly greased loaf pan—about 10x5x3 inches. Pour another can of tomato soup over the top. Bake in a moderate oven, 350 degrees, for 1 1/2 hours. Pour off juices before unmolding.

## Austrian Noodle Dish

1 pound of egg noodles
1 teaspoon cinnamon
2 or 3 eggs
Brown sugar to taste, about 2 or 3 tablespoons
1/4 cup chopped walnuts or other nuts
1/4 cup raisins
1 medium-sized grated apple
1 teaspoon salt
Butter or shortening

Cook the noodles in salted water to which the cinnamon has been added. Drain. Separate the eggs. Beat the whites until stiff and place them in the refrigerator while putting the rest of the dish together. Beat the egg yolks and add raisins, apple and nuts, and salt. Mix with noodles. Sweeten to taste with brown sugar. Slowly and gently fold in the beaten egg whites. Put in a greased casserole, and dot well over the top with butter. Bake in a moderate oven, 350 degrees, for about 1/2 hour or until brown on top.

## Mustard Ring

3/4 cup sugar
1 1/2 tablespoons dry mustard
2/3 cup cider vinegar
1/2 cup water
4 eggs
1 package unflavored gelatin
1 tablespoon cold water
1/2 pint whipping cream
Salt to taste

Mix dry ingredients and sift through a fine sieve. Add vinegar and water, then add the well-beaten eggs. Put the gelatin in the top of a double boiler with the tablespoon of cold water and stir vigorously over boiling water until gelatin melts. Add vinegar mixture slowly, stirring constantly and being careful to keep the gelatin in even distribution. When thoroughly mixed, remove from heat and set in cold water to cool. When mixture begins to show signs of setting, add whipping cream, not whipped. Add salt to taste and pour into either an oiled ring mold or one that has been rinsed with cold water. Chill until firm. Serves 6 to 8.

The center may be filled with shredded cabbage or cole slaw. This is good served with barbecue as well as ham dishes.

## Bittersweet Mint Pie

1 package of unflavored gelatin
1/2 cup milk
1 1/2 cups scalded milk
3/4 cup sugar
1 tablespoon cornstarch
3 egg yolks
2 squares of unsweetened chocolate
3 egg whites, beaten
1/2 cup cream, whipped
1/4 cup creme de menthe
1 9-inch baked pie crust with high fluted edge

Put the 1/2 cup cold milk in a bowl. Sprinkle the gelatin over the top. Scald the milk and add the sugar mixed with the cornstarch and beaten in with egg yolks. Add a little of the hot milk and blend until smooth. Add to the rest of the milk, and cook over hot water in a double boiler until the mixture coats the spoon. Add softened gelatin and chill until fairly firm. While this is being done, melt the chocolate over hot water and set aside to cool.

Beat the egg whites until stiff. When custard is chilled, stir to make it smooth and fluffy and then fold in the beaten egg whites. When thoroughly blended, fold in the 1/2 cup cream, whipped.

Divide the custard in half. Add melted, cooked chocolate to one half, and the creme de menthe plus a drop or two of green food coloring to the other half. Place chocolate layer in the bottom of your baked and cooled pastry shell, and top with the mint half. Then chill. Serve topped with grated chocolate and whipped cream.

# Shaker Seasoning

The Shaker tradition of fine food is much in evidence at Shakertown at Pleasant Hill, just down the road from Harrodsburg, Ky. Here is a sampling of dishes from the menu offered by the Trustees' House dining rooms, all with the simple goodness that characterizes Shaker cooking.

### Chicken Keene

A 4- or 5-pound hen, cooked
2 teaspoons salt
1/8 teaspoon pepper
1/3 cup butter or margarine
1/3 cup flour
1 cup chicken broth
1 1/2 cups milk or light cream
1/2 pound mushrooms, sliced and sauteed
1 pimiento, cut up in strips
1 large green pepper, cut in strips and blanched
Sherry to taste

Skin and bone chicken; cut meat in fairly large pieces; chill. Melt butter in top of a double boiler and stir in the flour. Slowly add the chicken broth and milk. Cook until thickened, while stirring. Add chicken, salt and pepper. Add mushrooms, pimiento, green pepper and sherry. Heat; season further. Garnish with paprika or minced parsley.

### Tomato-Celery Soup

1 small onion, chopped
2 tablespoons butter
1 10 1/2-ounce can tomato soup
1 soup can water
1 teaspoon minced parsley
1/2 cup finely chopped celery
1 tablespoon lemon juice
1 teaspoon sugar
1/4 teaspoon salt
1/8 teaspoon pepper

Brown onion in the butter, add remaining ingredients and simmer 5 minutes. Celery will remain crisp. Serves 6.

### Shaker Daily Loaf

*(Four 1-pound loaves)*

2 cups milk
1/4 cup sugar
4 teaspoons salt
8 tablespoons shortening
2 cups water
1 cake yeast
1/4 cup lukewarm water
12 cups sifted flour (about)

Scald milk and add sugar, salt and shortening. After shortening melts add water and cool to lukewarm. Add yeast, softened in the lukewarm water (105 degrees to 115 degrees). Add flour gradually, mixing it in thoroughly. When dough is stiff, turn it onto a lightly floured board and knead until smooth and satiny. Shape into a smooth ball, place in greased bowl, cover and let rise in a warm place, until it almost doubles in bulk. Divide into 4 equal portions, round up each into a smooth ball. Cover well and let rest for 10 to 15 minutes. Flatten out well and fold lengthwise. Stretch dough, fold ends together. Fold lengthwise and fold lengthwise once again. Roll and put in greased bread pans, seams towards bottom. Brush with melted butter or shortening. Let rise until double in bulk. Bake at 350 degrees for 20 minutes. If loaf shakes in pan and sounds hollow when it is thumped lightly, it is done. Let cool away from drafts. When cooled, wrap and store. Can be frozen.

### Pleasant Hill Baked Eggplant

1 large eggplant
1/2 medium onion
2 tablespoons butter
3 tablespoons chopped parsley
1 can cream of mushroom soup
Dash of Worcestershire sauce
Salt and pepper to taste
Butter crackers (not saltines)
Bits of butter for top

Cut off eggplant top, lengthwise, scrape out inside, leaving 1/4-inch around sides and bottom of shell. Boil the eggplant meat in salted water until it is tender. Drain thoroughly and chop. Saute the onion in butter and add chopped parsley. Mix with the eggplant and soup, then add enough crumbled crackers to make good stuffing consistency. Pile filling into eggplant shell, sprinkle more crumbs on top and dot with butter. Bake at 375 degrees for 30 to 35 minutes.

### Shaker Lemon Pie

Pastry for 2 crusts
2 lemons
2 cups sugar
4 eggs

Slice two lemons as thin as paper, rind and all. Place them in a bowl and put the sugar over them. Mix well and let stand for 2 hours or more. Beat the eggs together and pour over lemons. Fill unbaked pie shell with mixture and add top crust. Cut small vents in the top crust to let out steam. Place in a pre-heated 450-degree oven for 15 minutes and then turn heat down to 350 degrees and bake for 30 minutes, or until a silver knife inserted into the custard comes out clean.

# Hot Brown How-to

The phenomenon of the Hot Brown Sandwich persists. Sometimes you won't hear it mentioned for a year. Then suddenly it comes into vogue again and everybody's looking for the recipe. In case you're not familiar with the Hot Brown, it consists of sliced chicken or turkey on toast, with Béchamel and Mornay sauces, garnished with crisp bacon.

## Hot Brown Sandwich

Simmer a hen in water seasoned with a few peppercorns, salt and bay leaf. When tender, cool in the broth. After cooling, cut the breast into thin slices.

### *Béchamel Sauce*

1/3 cup butter or margarine
1/2 medium-sized sliced onion, minced
1/3 cup flour
3 cups hot milk
1 teaspoon salt
Dash of red pepper
Sprigs of parsley (optional)
Dash of nutmeg

Melt the butter or margarine in a saucepan. Add onion and cook slowly until light brown, about 15 or 20 minutes. Add flour and blend until the flour makes a smooth paste with the onion minces in it. Add milk and other seasonings and cook, stirring constantly and briskly until the sauce is thick and smooth. Then continue to cook, stirring occasionally, about 25 minutes altogether. Strain. If the sauce isn't to be used immediately, stir occasionally to keep a crust from forming on the top.

### *Mornay Sauce*

2 cups of Bechamel Sauce
2 egg yolks
1/2 cup grated Parmesan cheese
1 tablespoon butter or margarine
4 tablespoons whipped cream

Heat the Bechamel Sauce and combine with egg yolks. Stir constantly and remove from heat as soon as it starts to boil. When hot and thick, add cheese and the butter or margarine. The sauce must not boil or it will curdle.

Then, for every 1/2 cup sauce that is to be used for the sandwich, fold in 1 tablespoon of whipped cream. Here, it would be 4 tablespoons.

Fry as many strips of bacon as the number of sandwiches you are fixing. Saute a mushroom cap for each sandwich.

To assemble, cut the crusts off 2 slices of bread for each sandwich and toast them. Put 1 slice of toast in an oven-proof shallow dish. Lay the slices of chicken on top of the toast. Cover with a heaping portion of the sauce. Place in a very hot oven or under the broiler until the sauce takes on the glow of a suntan. Cut the extra slice of toast diagonally, and put the tips at each end. Top with bacon strip and the mushroom.

A little more grated cheese mixed with bread crumbs can be sprinkled over the sauce.

## Salad Dressing

1 tablespoon dry mustard
1 tablespoon Worcestershire sauce
2 teaspoons salt
1/4 teaspoon paprika
1/4 teaspoon black pepper
1/2 cup sugar
1 1/2 cups salad oil
1/2 cup wine vinegar or regular vinegar
1/4 cup cider vinegar
1 can condensed tomato soup

Measure ingredients into a bowl. Beat with egg beater until well-blended. Pour into 2 pint jars, one for now, one to keep in reserve. To one jar add 1 teaspoon onion juice and 1 clove garlic peeled and gashed, for today's salad.

## Fruit Bowl Elegance

1 can each of pitted Bing cherries and Royal Ann cherries
1 medium-sized fresh pineapple
1 pint of strawberries
Syrup from the white cherries
Sugar
Rum (optional)

Mix both kinds of cherries and the chunked pineapple together. Flavor about half of the syrup from the white cherries with rum to taste; if you don't use the rum, flavor the juice with a little sugar and lemon juice to taste. Pour this over the three fruits and put in the refrigerator to chill. Have enough juice but not so much to drown the fruits.

Wash and clean strawberries and sprinkle lightly with sugar. Slice. Add these to the other fruit just before serving.

# Campfire Cookery

It is an open secret that autumn is the loveliest time of all for a camping trip. A glorious stew simmering over an open fire feeds body and soul. Here's Paprika Camp Stew, then, and other nourishments for the outdoorsman.

### Paprika Camp Stew

1/4 cup shortening or oil
3 pounds lean beef cut in large chunks
8 potatoes, peeled and left whole
8 medium onions, peeled and left whole
4 stalks celery, sliced
6 carrots, sliced
1 tablespoon paprika
Salt and pepper to taste
2 tablespoons cornstarch mixed with 2 tablespoons water
1 small can peas, drained
1 cup sour cream (optional)

Heat shortening and brown the meat quickly. Remove meat from pan and add the potatoes and onions. Sprinkle with the paprika and stir for a nice red coat. Place the browned meat on top of the onions and potatoes and add the celery and carrots. Add salt and pepper. Add water to within an inch of top of pan. Cover and simmer slowly for 1 1/2 to 2 hours, adding water as necessary. When vegetables are tender, add the cornstarch-water mixture and blend well. Cook until gravy is clear and thickened. Add peas and sour cream. Stir just enough

to blend and serve hot. Vary proportions of celery, carrots and onions according to your favorites and omit a vegetable if it is unliked. But remember that many vegetables, unpopular with your family, chopped fine, will "disappear" after long simmering.

### Hot Fruit Dumplings

1 large can (1 pound, 14 ounces) sliced peaches or
   cherries (not pie filling)
1/4 cup butter
1/4 cup sugar
1/4 teaspoon salt
1/4 teaspoon cinnamon (optional)
1 1/2 cups biscuit mix
2 tablespoons sugar
1/2 cup plus 1 tablespoon milk or water

Heat fruit to boiling in heavy skillet or Dutch oven. Stir in the butter, sugar, salt and cinnamon. Blend biscuit mix with the sugar and milk or water. Drop by spoonfuls on top of hot fruit. Reduce heat and cook 10 minutes uncovered, then put on the lid and cook about 10 minutes covered, or until dumplings are cooked through. 4 to 6 servings.

### Breakfast Eggs on Rice

This is not so much a recipe as it is an interesting idea: After you've cooked your bacon or sausage in a heavy skillet or Dutch oven, remove meat and keep it warm. Pour off the fat, leaving the brownings in the pan. Then, to serve 6 people, assemble these ingredients:

1 1/2 cups minute rice
1 1/2 cups hot water or broth
1/2 teaspoon salt
6 eggs
Tabasco sauce
6 teaspoons butter

Stir the dry rice into the brown skillet leavings. Add the water and salt, and cover. Cook over very low heat 5 minutes. Now make 6 indentations in the level bed of rice and break an egg into each hole. Put a drop of Tabasco and dab of butter on top of each egg. Cover and cook slowly for another 5 minutes or so, or until eggs are done to suit.

# A Bounteous Buffet

The most elegantly furnished buffet isn't necessarily the costliest, as witness Ballotines de Vol-aille. For a pre-theatre dinner, set it for an early hour; the buffet is a dramatic production it-self, and the temptation is to linger.

### Ballottines de Volaille

Buy one large chicken leg (with thigh attached) per person to be served. If the butcher won't bone them, here's how: Place chicken leg on board, skin side down. With a very sharp knife, slit meat down both sides of bone. With the knife bearing against bone at all times, work and scrape meat away from the bone, taking care not to cut through the skin. You may mangle the flesh some, but get the bone out and keep the skin intact. Now, put boned chicken pieces between sheets of waxed paper and flatten them with a foil-wrapped brick. They should spread out to about 6 by 8 inches. May be refrigerated, wrapped, overnight, before stuffing and finishing.

### Duxelle Stuffing

1/2 stick butter
1 tablespoon finely minced shallots (or substitute green onion)
1/2 pound mushrooms, finely chopped
1 pound lean veal, finely ground
Juice of 1 lemon
1 cup dry white wine
1 1/2 cups fine white bread crumbs
2 eggs, beaten
Salt and pepper
(Rosemary and salt for the chicken)

Heat butter to foaming in heavy pan. Add shallots, mushrooms and veal. Cook and stir 5 minutes, breaking up the meat thoroughly. Add lemon juice and wine and cook over medium heat until liquid is reduced by more than half. Remove from heat and add the crumbs and beaten eggs. Season to taste with salt and pepper.

To stuff: Sprinkle each piece of chicken sparingly with salt and dried rosemary. (Break up the rosemary, or powder it, and use less than 1/8 teaspoon per chicken leg, as it is extremely flavorful.) This stuffing will fill 8 legs plumply, or up to 12 less amply. Place filling on meat and roll up, making sure it's all encased in skin. Use wooden picks to fasten if you think they may unroll while baking. Place, open side down, in shallow pan and bake 1 hour at 350 degrees, basting occasionally with pan juices. Keep hot, while sauce is made. Serve on prepared croutons, using a well warmed platter, and top with wine-butter sauce.

### Wine-Butter Sauce

After removing chicken from pan, "wash" pan with a cup dry white wine, scraping the browned particles loose. Put the goodies from this process in a saucepan and add 2 tablespoons shallots, finely chopped. Cook until liquid is reduced by half. Stir in 1/2-stick of butter, salt and pepper to taste, and a teaspoon of lemon juice. Strain if you wish. Spoon over the hot ballottines.

### To Make Croutons

Trim crusts from a loaf of unsliced bread, then slice 2/3- to 3/4-inch thick. Melt a stick of butter and dip one side of each slice in butter. Place on baking sheet and bake at 300 degrees until lightly browned, about 30 minutes. May be made ahead of time and reheated.

### Deep Purple Salad

2 3-ounce packages raspberry gelatin
2 jars (1 pound, 1 ounce each) boysenberries
3 (1/2 pint) cartons sour cream
3/4 cup chopped pecans or English walnuts
1 cup juice from berries, boiling hot
1 teaspoon plain gelatin softened in 1 tablespoon juice

Drain boysenberries, reserving juice. Measure 1 cup juice and bring to boiling. Use 1 tablespoon juice to soften the teaspoon plain gelatin. Pour hot juice over raspberry gelatin, stir to dissolve, and stir in the softened plain gelatin. Chill until syrupy, then add boysenberries, sour cream and nuts. Pour into a 2-quart mold and chill until firm. Unmold on crisp greens. 12 servings.

*Continued*

## Sweet Green Peas

1 cup water
1/4 cup sugar
2 teaspoons salt
3 10 1/2-ounce packages frozen peas
1 stick (1/2-cup) butter

Put water, sugar and salt in saucepan and bring to boil, covered. Add peas and cook uncovered 8 to 10 minutes, until just tender. Drain; season with butter. 8 to 10 servings.

## Paris Brest

1 baked 10-inch ring of chou (cream puff) paste with almonds (recipe follows)
1 box custard mix
3/4 cup good strawberry jam or perserves
2 1/2 or 3 little sponge cakes ("mary janes")
1/4 cup triple sec or kirsch liqueur
1 cup heavy cream, whipped
3 tablespoons powdered sugar, sifted over top for garnish, if desired

Make up the custard according to package directions, but use only 1 1/2 cups milk. Cool thoroughly. Split top from chou ring carefully, setting top aside. Remove any doughy particles. Spread bottom with strawberry jam. Soak the sponge cakes, which have been halved down through the middle, in the liqueur and place them over the jam, trimming them to fit. Add the custard, then the whipped cream. Fit top of ring over the whipped cream and sift powdered sugar liberally over the top. Makes 12 servings.

## Chou (Cream Puff) Pastry Ring

3/4 cup water
3/4 stick butter
3/4 cup flour
3 eggs
1/4 cup slivered almonds

Boil water and butter until butter is melted. Add flour all at once; stir over medium heat until mixture clings to spoon in a firm ball. Remove from heat and beat in eggs, singly, making sure each is blended before adding another. Make a circle on an ungreased baking sheet, using 9-inch cake pan for pattern, marking with a buttered finger. Spoon paste over guideline, forming solid ring, leaving open space in center 3 or 4 inches across. Sprinkle almonds on top. Bake at 425 degrees 15 minutes, reduce heat to 350 degrees; bake about 30 minutes longer, until deep brown. Prick ring in several places with knife tip, and let stand in oven with heat off and door open for 5 minutes.

# die Deutsche Küche

From Southern Germany comes Gefülte Pfanküchen — stuffed pancakes — with a savory meat stuffing and a topping of Swiss cheese and sour cream. German from start to finish, this dinner for eight has everything, and can even include steins of beer alongside!

### Gefülte Pfanküchen

*Pancake batter: (makes 10 pancakes)*

> 6 eggs, beaten
> 1 cup flour
> 1/2 cup milk

Beat milk and flour into the beaten eggs. Heat an 8-inch skillet and pour in just enough batter (1/4 to 1/3 cup) to make a very, very thin covering on the bottom. When baked on one side, carefully turn and bake on the other side. The thinness of the pancakes is important, so rotate the skillet when you pour in the batter so that only the bottom is coated. As the cakes are prepared, keep them on a warm platter until ready to fill with:

> 2 pounds ground round
> 2 eggs
> 3 teaspoons salt, and pepper to taste
> 2 teaspoons ground nutmeg
> 1 teaspoon monosodium glutamate
> 1/4 cup fine dry bread crumbs
> 1/4 cup each chopped onion and parsley
> 1/2 cup milk

Add ½ cup milk to make the mixture resemble meat loaf, but thinner, so it will spread. Spread rounded 1/3 cup meat mixture on each pancake, roll up and place in shallow casserole. Allow one roll per person. When all rolls are laid into baking pan, top with: 1 pound slivered Swiss cheese. Pour over the casserole:

> 2 cups sour cream, mixed with
> 3/4 cup milk

Bake at 350 degrees until hot and bubbly.

### Red Cabbage

> 1 medium head of red cabbage, shredded
> 1 rounded tablespoon shortening
> 1/2 cup vinegar
> 1 teaspoon salt
> 1/2 cup sugar

Remove outer leaves and shred cabbage from stalk. Melt shortening in iron kettle. Add the cabbage and the rest of the ingredients. Cook gently till tender, about two hours. Taste and add a bit more salt if needed.

### Cucumbers with Mustard Dressing

> 3 large cucumbers, pared and sliced thin
> 2 tablespoons oil
> 4 tablespoons vinegar
> 1 tablespoon prepared mustard
> 1 teaspoon salt, and pepper to taste

Place sliced cucumbers in a bowl and cover with ice. When ready to serve, drain and mix well with the other ingredients which have been combined thoroughly. Serve on lettuce or simply in little sauce dishes.

### Hazelnuss Torte

> 1/2 pound finely grated hazelnuts (filberts)
> 2 large apples, or 3 smaller ones, peeled and grated
> 6 eggs, separated
> 1 cup sugar

Beat the egg yolks together with the sugar until very light. Add the grated nuts and apples, mixing thoroughly. Fold in the stiffly beaten egg whites. Pour into well-greased 9-inch cake pan and bake 45 minutes at 325 degrees.

# Veal and Stuff

Succulent, delicate veal has not often been used to better advantage than this: Sausage, fresh pork, and herbs are rolled up inside, to point up the flavor. A cheerful red line of pimiento edges the stuffing when the roast is sliced. Cooks' reputations have been made on lesser dinners!

## Stuffed Veal

5 to 6 pounds of veal leg, boned and flattened by the butcher
1/2 pound fresh pork
1/2 pound mild pork sausage
1/2 pound coarse dry-bread crumbs
1 egg
2 teaspoons salt
1/2 teaspoon pepper
2 tablespoons dried or chopped fresh parsley
2 teaspoons crushed dried or fresh tarragon
2 tablespoons chopped chives
2 six-ounce cans pimiento

Rub the meat on both sides with the salt, pepper and tarragon. To prepare the stuffing, put the ground meats in a large bowl with the bread crumbs, egg, parsley and chives. Mix with the hands, adding boiling water until the proper consistency for spreading is reached.

Drain the pimientos, open them up flat and use them to cover the inside of the meat. Spread the prepared stuffing over the pimientos.

Roll up the meat and fasten the seam securely. A neat closure is assured if you work in a row of metal skewers and, with heavy string, pretend you are lacing a huge stuffed shoe—crossing the string around the ends of the skewers and pulling tight between, with a knot at the finish.

Preheat the oven to 325 degrees. Place the meat on a foil-lined flat baking pan and roast uncovered for 3 to 4 hours, or until very tender and well done. Veal must be well done, and especially in this recipe, with a pork-laden interior.

Moist heat and added fat are usually needed in roasting veal, but the dressing will supply both. Lay a loose bonnet of foil over the roast after it has browned sufficiently, to prevent further crusting over and give a bit of extra steam. This roast is lovely when sliced, with its red line of pimiento defining the circles of stuffing.

## Fresh Brussels Sprouts

Like any member of the cabbage family, the fresh Brussels sprout should have a 15-minute bath in salted water before cooking, to flush out any hidden cabbage worm. Rinse the sprouts well and boil gently in salted water for 15 or 20 minutes. Two pounds of fresh Brussels sprouts will make about 8 servings. Three packages of frozen sprouts give the same yield. Spoon hollandaise over hot vegetable just before serving.

## Blender Hollandaise

1/4 pound butter or margarine
4 egg yolks
2 tablespoons lemon juice
1/4 teaspoon salt
Pinch of cayenne

In a small saucepan, heat butter just to bubbling. Meanwhile, put egg yolks, lemon juice, salt and cayenne into container of electric blender. Cover container; turn blender on high speed. Immediately remove cover and add hot butter in steady stream. To keep, store in refrigerator. Makes 1 1/4 cups sauce. To use it after storing, let it come to room temperature, spoon it on the hot vegetable and it will melt.

## Colonial Bread

3 tablespoons shortening
3 tablespoons sugar
4 1/2 teaspoons baking powder
3 cups whole-wheat flour (or graham flour)
1 1/2 cups white flour
2 1/4 cups milk
1 1/2 teaspoons salt
1 egg plus 1 egg yolk

Cream shortening with sugar. Beat in egg and yolk. Sift together white flour, salt and baking powder. Add alternately with milk to the egg mixture. Stir in graham or whole-wheat flour, gently but thoroughly. Divide batter between

*Continued*

two 1-pound loaf pans, well greased. Let stand 20 minutes, before baking at 350 degrees for 45 to 50 minutes.

## Green and White Noodles

6 oz. green noodles
6 oz. white noodles
1/4 cup butter or margarine
1/4 cup milk
1/2 teaspoon basil (optional)
3 tablespoons Parmesan cheese

Bring to a full rolling boil 3 quarts of water in each of two separate saucepans. Put 2 teaspoons of salt in each pot. Cook green noodles in one, white noodles in the other, for about 10 to 15 minutes, or until tender enough for your taste. Drain and stir 2 tablespoons of butter or margarine and 2 tablespoons of milk into each. Lightly mix the two colors in serving dish and sprinkle a light dusting of Parmesan cheese on top.

## Country Gazpacho

4 cups ripe tomatoes
3 cups fresh cucumbers
1 cup onion
Salt and pepper to taste
1/4 cup hot bacon drippings or olive oil (see note below)

Pare and cube all the vegetables small. Mix together with the salt and pepper. Just before serving, stir in the hot bacon drippings. This is best served in small sauce bowls with its own liquid. Use a spoon instead of salad forks, as most people want to consume the remaining liquid, too. In fact, this dish makes an excellent and appetizing first course as a soup. Serves 8.

Note: If you want it chilled, season it with olive oil. Bacon grease will congeal if poured on ice-cold vegetables, so have the vegetables at room temperature.

## Cream Puff Vesuvius

1 cup water
1/2 cup butter (1 stick)
1 cup flour
4 eggs

Place water and butter in a heavy saucepan and bring to a rolling boil. Add the flour all at once and stir hard with a wooden spoon over medium heat until the mixture clings to the spoon in a ball. Remove from heat and put in large bowl of electric mixer. At medium speed, beat smooth, then add the eggs one at a time, beating for a full minute after each addition. The batter should be very stiff.

With a teaspoon, make walnut-size puffs two inches apart on an ungreased cookie sheet. Bake at 400 degrees for 25-30 minutes until lightly browned. Turn off oven and, with the oven door open, leave the puffs in the diminishing heat for 5 minutes. Remove from pan with spatula and cut a slit in the side of each puff so steam can escape. When cold fill with:

## Chipped Chocolate Cream

2 cups whipping cream, whipped
1 teaspoon vanilla
2 squares sweet baking chocolate, shaved or chopped
1/4 cup sugar

Fold the sugar gradually into the whipped cream, then add vanilla and shaved chocolate, folding to blend. Spoon the whipped cream into the split puffs.

It's easy to build a tower of the filled puffs: Boil together 1/2 cup water and 1/2 cup sugar until it becomes a heavy syrup. Cool. Spoon a little syrup on the bottom of the serving plate to anchor the arrangement, and place cream puffs in a circle on the plate, filling in the center of the circle, too.

Dip the bottom of the remaining puffs, one at a time, into the syrup and build them, tier on tier, into a high-rise confection. Sift a little powdered sugar over the top. Melt a square of sweet chocolate, stir in 2 tablespoons of boiling water, and drizzle this over the top. Eight to 10 servings.

# Turkey-Day Dinner

Turkey is still king at Thanksgiving time; tradition decrees it. Yet there's every reason to improve and enlarge on tradition. The old-fashioned paper bag method of roasting turkey is wonderful in its simplicity. Another golden oldie is Indian Pudding for dessert, but there's a lot that's new in this menu, too.

## Sour Cream Bisque

1/2 cup butter (1 stick)
2 cans (8 ounces) sliced mushrooms, drained
2 cloves garlic, minced
1/2 teaspoon thyme
4 cans (11 ounces each) condensed bisque of tomato soup
1 cup sour cream
4 cups water
Chopped chives or parsley

In saucepan, melt butter, sauté mushrooms, garlic and thyme. Add soup and sour cream; gradually stir in water. Heat to serving temperature, stirring occasionally. Garnish with chives or parsley.

## Turkey Roasted in a Paper Bag

Thaw turkey, remove and wash giblets, and put them in a large pan to cook separately. Wash and dry turkey. Rub bird all over with cooking oil or soft butter. Mix together 1 teaspoon each salt and flour per 5 pounds of turkey and rub mixture on inside and outside of the turkey. Truss neatly; do not stuff. Place bird in brown paper bag and fold the end tightly, fastening with paper clips or safety pins. Any sort of sturdy brown bag will do. It is worth noting that a 20-pound turkey (no larger) will fit into the largest-size standard bag from the grocery store. Preheat oven and roast at 300 degrees, timed according to the instructions on this chart:

7-10 pounds, 30 minutes per pound

10-15 pounds, 20 minutes per pound

15-18 pounds, 18 minutes per pound

18-20 pounds, 15 minutes per pound

20-23 pounds, 13 minutes per pound

At the end of the cooking time, remove from oven and let stand 10 minutes before opening bag. Cut away top of bag and remove turkey to warm platter. Make gravy from the rich juices left in the bottom of the bag.

If you set the giblets to simmering, covered, on the back of the stove when you put in the turkey, they should be done and ready to be chopped and added to gravy.

## Chestnut Dressing

1 9-inch square pan corn bread, made from mix or your favorite recipe
6 cups dry bread cubes
2 teaspoons salt
1/8 teaspoon pepper
1/2 teaspoon sweet basil
1 teaspoon sage
1/2 teaspoon marjoram
1 cup chopped onion
2 cups chopped celery
1 pound chestnuts, cooked, hulled and sliced
1/4 cup butter or margarine
2 eggs, beaten
1 cup or more chicken or turkey stock

Combine crumbled corn bread, bread cubes, salt, pepper, basil, sage and marjoram in large bowl. Saute onion, celery and chestnuts lightly in butter and add to bread mixture. Add eggs and stock, mixing lightly. Add more stock to get the desired consistency. Grease a large (3-or-4 quart) flat casserole and, using an ice cream scoop, place balls of dressing in it. Bake, lightly covered with foil, for about an hour at 350 degrees. Remove foil to brown dressing.

## Sweet Potato Nut Balls

Combine 1½ cups mashed sweet potatoes, ¼ cup orange juice and 2 tablespoons sugar. Blend well. Shape sweet potato mixture into 12 balls using approximately 2 tablespoons for each ball. Roll the sweet potato balls in chopped pecans. Place on a cookie sheet and heat in a moderate oven, (350 degrees) 15 to 20 minutes or until heated through. Yield: 12 sweet potato balls.

## Spicy Cranberry Relish

4 cups raw cranberries
1 cup sugar
1 cup port or sherry wine
1/2 cup water
1 stick whole cinnamon
4 whole cloves
4 thin slices lemon
1/8 teaspoon salt

Pick over cranberries; wash and drain. Bring sugar, wine, water and spices to a boil and simmer for 5 minutes. Add lemon, salt and cranberries, and continue cooking until skins pop, about 5 minutes. Cool. Makes about 1 quart.

*Continued*

## Corn-Oyster Bake

2 cans (10 oz. each) frozen condensed oyster stew
1 can (1 lb. 1 oz.) cream-style corn
1 can (1 lb. 1 oz.) whole-kernel golden corn, drained
1 1/4 crushed cracker crumbs
1 egg, slightly beaten
1/2 teaspoon salt
Dash seasoned pepper
2 tablespoons pimiento, chopped
1/4 cup onion, chopped
1 teaspoon parsley, chopped
1/4 teaspoon ground sage
2 tablespoons butter or margarine, melted
1/2 cup cracker crumbs

Thaw oyster stew by placing unopened cans in hot water for 10 minutes. Combine stew, cream-style corn, whole-kernel corn, 1¼ cups cracker crumbs, egg, seasonings, pimiento, parsley and onion. Pour into greased 2-quart casserole. Combine melted butter or margarine and ½ cup cracker crumbs; sprinkle on top of corn mixture. Bake in moderate (350-degree) oven for 1 hour or until knife inserted halfway between center and edge comes out clean. Serves 8 to 10.

## Glacéed Vegetable Paradise

2 (10 oz.) packages broccoli spears
2 (2 lb.) cans whole tomatoes
2 tablespoons butter or margarine
4 teaspoons flour
2 teaspoons minced onion
1/2 cup cracker crumbs
2 tablespoons butter or margarine
1/4 cup grated Parmesan cheese

Cook broccoli, according to package directions, until almost done. Drain tomatoes, reserving liquid. Melt butter; stir in flour and onion. Slowly add reserved tomato liquid and cook, stirring constantly, until thickened. Drain broccoli and place in the center of a shallow casserole dish. Slice tomatoes in half, crosswise, and place decoratively around broccoli. Spoon sauce over vegetables and top with cracker crumbs that have been sautéed in butter. Sprinkle with Parmesan cheese. Bake at 350 degrees for 30 minutes. Makes 12 servings.

## Durgin Park Indian Pudding

1 cup yellow cornmeal
1/2 cup molasses
1/2 cup granulated sugar
1/4 cup butter or shortening
1/4 teaspoon salt
1/4 teaspoon baking soda
2 eggs
1 1/2 quarts hot milk

Mix all ingredients with one-half (¾ quart) of hot milk and bake in very hot oven until it boils. Then stir well and add remaining hot milk. Bake in slow oven, for five or more hours —perhaps seven hours. (Bake in stone crock, well greased). Stir at invervals. The secret of its excellence lies in slow and careful cooking. Top with ice cream or whipped cream. 12 servings.

R. BRIGGS

# The Pies Have It!

When in doubt, serve pie. Because pie, of one kind or another, is everybody's favorite dessert. Here are the Ultimate Ones, for those who simply cannot resist a heavenly, rich pastry. Don't even try to decide among them; try them all.

## Curaçao Marmalade Pie

Pastry for 9-inch, 2-crust pie
2 oranges
1/2 cup water
1 1/4 cups sugar
2 1/2 tablespoons cornstarch
1/4 cup soft butter
Juice of 1/2 lemon
3 eggs (reserve 1 teaspoon yolk to brush top crust)
1 teaspoon water (mix with teaspoon egg yolk)
2 tablespoons Curaçao liqueur

Wash and dry oranges. Pare off, paper thin, only the bright part of skins, using potato parer. Grind or chop fine the rind. Section the oranges, then squeeze out all remaining juice. Combine ground peel, orange sections and juice, lemon juice, ¼ cup of the sugar and the water. Boil gently 15 minutes and cool.

Meanwhile, combine 1 cup sugar with the cornstarch. Cream in the butter. Beat in eggs, one at a time. Add cooled marmalade mixture and Curaçao. Pour into prepared unbaked crust. Roll out top crust and cut out designs or slits for steam to escape. Brush with the teaspoon of egg yolk and water. Put top crust on pie and seal to bottom crust. Sprinkle with a little sugar.

Bake 10 minutes at 425 degrees, then 45 minutes at 350 degrees. Serve at room temperature.

## Apricot Fried Pies

First, prepare baking-powder biscuit dough.

*Filling:*

2 cups cooked, dried apricots
3/4 cup sugar
1/4 teaspoon cinnamon

Roll biscuit dough thin, about 1/8 of an inch. Using a saucer as a pattern, cut circles of dough. Moisten edge of circles with water so they'll stick together when folded. Put 1 to 2 tablespoons of fruit filling on each circle and seal edges by crimping with a fork.

Use a slotted spoon to lower the pies into hot inch-deep fat. Fry till golden brown. Drain on absorbent paper. Serve warm, sprinkled with powdered sugar.

## Almond and Coconut Tarts

Have ready: 10 baked plain pastry tart shells.

*Basic cream pie filling:*

1/2 cup sugar
4 tablespoons cornstarch
2 cups milk
3 egg yolks, slightly beaten
1 tablespoon butter

Mix sugar and cornstarch in heavy-bottomed saucepan. Gradually add milk and cook, stirring constantly, until thick. Pour half the hot mixture slowly into the beaten egg yolks, return all to saucepan and stir over low heat just 3 or 4 minutes to finish cooking the egg yolks. Stir in butter. Cool.

Divide the filling in half. To one half, add ½ teaspoon almond extract. To the other half, add ½ teaspoon vanilla and ½ cup coconut. Makes 5 almond and 5 coconut tarts. Fill baked tart shells.

Make tall pyramids of meringue (recipe follows) on filling, sealing to the edges of the crust. Sprinkle almond-flavored tarts with slivered almonds, and the coconut filling with coconut. Bake 5 minutes at 400 degrees, or until golden.

*Meringue:* Beat 5 egg whites until almost stiff. On low speed of mixer, gradually add 10 tablespoons sugar, beating until glossy stiff. Stir in 1 teaspoon vanilla. Pile onto filling.

## Winner's Circle Pie

1 cup chocolate chips
1 cup English walnuts
2 eggs, beaten
1 cup sugar
1 stick butter, melted and cooled
1/2 cup flour
1 teaspoon vanilla

Mix sugar and flour, add eggs and then butter. Add English walnuts and chocolate chips and vanilla. Pour into unbaked pie shell and bake 30 minutes at 350 degrees. Test with a toothpick. Bake longer if necessary—it should be chewy, not runny.

*Continued*

## Cherry Tiny Tarts

*Cookie pastry:*

>1 cup butter
>1 cup powdered sugar
>1 egg plus one egg yolk
>2 2/3 cups flour
>1 teaspoon salt
>1 teaspoon vanilla

Cream together the butter and sugar. Beat in the vanilla, egg and yolk. Blend in the flour and salt which have been sifted or stirred together. Shape into a roll 2 inches in diameter, wrap in waxed paper and freeze. Freezing makes the pastry easy to handle.

Slice 1/4- to 1/3-inch thick. With floured fingertips press into bottoms and halfway up the sides of tiny tart pans, having the pastry a bit thicker on the bottom than on the sides.

*Cherry filling:*

>3/4 cup good cherry preserves
>1/2 cup finely grated almonds
>1/4 cup butter
>1 egg
>1/2 teaspoon almond extract
>1/4 cup sugar

Beat the egg in a mixer and mix in the rest of the ingredients. The cherries should be mashed to a pulp. Put 1 1/2 teaspoons of filling into each pastry-lined little tin. Bake at 350 degrees for 20 minutes. Cool a few minutes in tins, then loosen with a tip of a sharp knife and slide the tarts out on racks to cool. Sprinkle with powdered sugar. Makes about 5 dozen tiny tarts.

## Gertrude's Lemon Chess Pie

>2 cups sugar
>4 eggs
>1/8 teaspoon salt
>2 tablespoons grated lemon rind
>1 tablespoon flour
>1 tablespoon corn meal
>1/4 cup melted butter
>1/4 cup milk
>1/4 cup lemon juice

Mix in all dry ingredients together. Beat in the eggs thoroughly and add the butter, milk and other ingredients. Pour into prepared 9-inch pastry shell and bake at 350 degrees for 50 to 60 minutes, or until set.

## Georgia's Black Bottom Pie

*Graham-Cracker Crust:* Mix together 2 cups of fine graham-cracker crumbs, 1/3 cup melted butter or margarine, and 3 tablespoons sugar. Press firmly on bottom and sides of 9-inch pie pan. Bake at 400 degrees for 5 minutes. Cool.

*Filling, Part 1:*

>1 1/2 tablespoons cornstarch
>1/4 teaspoon salt
>1/2 cup sugar
>2 cups milk (let it be heating in heavy saucepan)
>3 egg yolks, beaten

Mix together the sugar, cornstarch, salt and egg yolks. Stir the hot milk slowly into the egg yolk mixture, return all to the heavy saucepan, and cook over low heat, stirring constantly until thick, about 15 minutes.

*Filling, Part 2:*

Melt 1½ squares unsweetened chocolate and add it to 1 cup of the Part 1 cooked mixture. Add 1 teaspoon vanilla. Pour into cooled pastry or graham-cracker crust. Refrigerate.

*Filling, Part 3:*

Take 1 envelope of gelatin and soak 3 minutes in 1/4 cup cold water. Add gelatin mixture to remaining cooked custard. Add 1 teaspoon vanilla. Chill in refrigerator while you beat 3 egg whites till foamy, adding ½ teaspoon cream of tartar. Continuing to beat, add ½ cup sugar gradually, and when stiff as meringue, fold into cooled gelatin-custard. Pour on top of chocolate layer in crust. Chill. Top with whipped cream and shaved unsweetened chocolate.

# A Herd of Turtles

A seven-gallon vat of turtle soup may not be the dish to whip up for just any old occasion. But if you have a multitude clamoring to be fed, here's the best turtle soup you can make. Serve it up with assorted breads and crackers, and crisp vegetable relishes.

### Turtle Soup (Makes Seven Gallons)

7 lbs. of turtle meat (amount can be filled out with some fresh beef tongue)
1/4 medium-size head of cabbage
6 medium-size carrots
1 pound fresh green beans
1 whole stalk or bunch celery
8 onions (about 2 1/2-inch diameter)
8 potatoes (about 3-inch diameter)
1 ten-ounce can tomato puree
3 lemons
6 hard-cooked eggs
2 No. 2 1/2 cans tomatoes (or 6 cups canned tomatoes)
1/2 cup whole allspice
1 can peas
2 ears of corn kernels (optional)
1 bottle catsup
1 red pepper
Salt to taste
1 cup browned flour
1 bottle claret
3 1/2 gallons of water (approximately)

Put turtle meat (or turtle and beef tongue) in cold water and allow to come slowly to a boil. Turn down heat and simmer gently until the meat is falling-apart tender. Turtle cooks more quickly than tongue, but as a cooking-time guide allow at least 2½ to 3½ hours to cook the meat.

While the meat is cooking, prepare the vegetables and get the seasonings ready. When meat has cooked, lift from broth, remove bones and trim the tongue, if used. Next, everything but the red pepper must go through the meat chopper; the canned tomato ingredients, corn, peas, 5 of the 6 eggs and 2 of the 3 lemons. The extra hard-cooked egg and lemon will be sliced for a garnish.

If you wait to chop until the meat is cooked, some of the easy-to-grind vegetables help the meat and softer vegetables through the chopper. The celery and carrots are excellent grinding helpers. Use either the medium or the fine knife. The grinding gauge should not have an opening larger than ¼ inch. Save all juice that drips from the grinder and put it with the other ground ingredients back into the stock.

To brown the flour, put it in a shallow pan under the broiler. Stir frequently to avoid lumping and scorching. Get a good brown tinge but don't let the flour burn.

Add catsup and red pepper. Add some salt, but not too much—wait till the last to judge seasoning. Tie the allspice in a cloth or small bag and toss it into the pot. Add sliced lemon and simmer all together for approximately 4 more hours. If additional water is needed use boiling water.

Fifteen minutes before serving, combine browned flour with cold water to make a smooth paste. Slowly stir in only enough to give body to soup. Simmer, stirring constantly for ten minutes. Turn off heat and stir in claret, just before serving. Garnish with hard-cooked egg.

# Culinary History

This dinner, to commemorate the Centenary Year of Pewee Valley, Ky., consists of dishes that would have been served when the town was chartered 100 years earlier, in 1870. The setting was the historic home of Annie Fellows Johnston, author of "The Little Colonel" books.

### Baked Country Ham

Select a well-shaped, blocky ham that is not too fat, of about 15 pounds. Scrub it well under running water and let it soak in warm water overnight.

Place ham in kettle, add water to cover and then add 1 cup red wine vinegar, a large potato cut in pieces and 1 cup dark brown sugar. Bring to a rolling boil, then reduce heat, cover and simmer for 20 minutes a pound. Let cool in its liquid.

With a thin, sharp carving knife, make stabs deep into the ham, pull knife handle back as far as possible and pour red wine vinegar into the holes made. When vinegar is absorbed, repeat several times, about 8 or 10 times for a 15-pound ham.

Remove skin and excess fat, if any. Score diagonally in opposite directions and rub with a mixture of dry mustard and dark brown sugar. Then stud with whole cloves.

Place ham in a roaster and bake uncovered at 350 degrees for 8 to 10 minutes per pound, or until nicely browned. Slice thinly and serve on beaten biscuit or "dolly" rolls.

### Turkey Hash

Stuffing: (Vary proportions to suit taste and size of the turkey.) Place bread crumbs in a large bowl. Fry and crumble sausage meat and remove from fat in pan. Fry chopped celery in the fat until transparent and remove from fat. Fry chopped onions in the fat until transparent and remove from fat. Fry sliced mushrooms in the fat.

Pour these over bread crumbs, add salt and pepper, toss well together. Beat eggs and add to dressing, together with parsley, poultry seasoning, thyme and marjoram to taste. Add hot water to make moist. Stuff both cavities of turkey.

Cover turkey with thin strips of beef suet and roast at 325 degrees for 25 to 30 minutes per pound, or until very tender. Cool. Strip all meat from the bones, dice meat and combine it with the dressing and the fats and juices in the roaster.

Place carcass with neck and giblets in a large kettle with water, salt and onion, to make broth. Cook until giblets are tender. Chop them, along with the neck meat, and add to the hash, along with broth, to make the desired consistency. Reheat, stirring well to mix all ingredients. Transfer to chafing dish or other serving piece, and serve over Lacey Cakes.

### Lacey Cakes

Sift together 2 cups white water-ground cornmeal, 1 teaspoon soda and 1 teaspoon salt. Slowly add 2 well-beaten eggs mixed with 2 1/2 cups buttermilk. Beat well until smooth. Drop by teaspoonfuls on hot, well-greased skillet, allowing 1 teaspoon lard for each 4 cakes. If batter gets too thick, thin with buttermilk, a tablespoon at a time.

### Spoon Bread

Pour 3 cups boiling water over 1 1/2 cups white water-ground cornmeal and boil, bubbling for 5 minutes, stirring constantly to prevent sticking. Remove from fire and add 1 1/2 tablespoons butter, 1 1/2 teaspoons salt and 3 egg yolks which have been beaten with 1 1/2 cups milk. Beat 3 egg whites and fold into the mixture. Pour into a well-greased baking dish and bake at 400 degrees for 30 minutes.

### Escalloped Oysters

Grease a 2-quart casserole well with butter. Place alternate layers of saltine crackers, coarsely crumbled, and fresh oysters in casserole, dotting each layer with butter and sprinkling lightly with pepper, until a quart of oysters, a large box of saltines and 1 pound of butter have been used.

Pour over all 1 pint of cream and any liquid from the oysters. Sprinkle with paprika and bake at 350 degrees for about 45 minutes, or until nicely browned.

*Continued*

## Pickled Carrots, Shaker Style

Cook 1 quart sliced carrots and 2 medium onions, sliced, in 1 cup water for about 10 minutes, so that they are not too done. Drain well. Then mix together:

    2 cups wine vinegar
    1 tablespoon olive oil
    3/4 cup sugar
    1 teaspoon salt
    1 teaspoon cinnamon
    1 teaspoon celery seed
    1/2 teaspoon ground ginger
    1/2 teaspoon ground cloves

Bring to a boil, reduce heat to simmering and add vegetables. Cook gently for 15 minutes. Cool and then chill thoroughly before serving.

## Pewee Valley Applesauce

Peel, core and slice 10 large Golden Delicious apples. Place in kettle with 1 1/2 cups water and cook, covered, for 10 minutes over low heat, stirring occasionally. Add 1 1/2 cups sugar and 1 teaspoon cinnamon and mix gently. Cook for about 5 minutes over medium heat. Cool and serve sprinkled with colored candy crystals.

## Candied Sweet Potatoes Lucifer

Cook 10 medium-sized sweet potatoes in their jackets in boiling water until almost done. Drain, peel and cut in slices about 1-inch thick. Place in buttered casserole. Combine and cook together for a few minutes:

    1 1/2 cups dark brown sugar
    1/2 cup water
    6 tablespoons butter
    1 tablespoon lemon juice

Pour this sauce over the potato slices and bake at 375 degrees for about 30 minutes. Baste occasionally. At serving time, you may flame them with a little brandy or Puerto Rican rum.

## Pewee Valley Stuffed Cucumbers

Cut unpeeled cucumbers in halves, lengthwise. Scoop out centers with a sharp spoon, being careful not to break shells. Grind scooped-out cucumber with green peppers, onion and parsley, using proportions to suit your taste. Season with salt, pepper and nutmeg and mix well. Stuff this mixture into shells. Sprinkle about 1 tablespoon dried bread crumbs over each half-cucumber and dot with butter.

Place in baking pan, add a little water to bottom of pan and bake at 350 degrees for about 45 minutes, or until well-browned.

## Centennial Salad Dressing

Place 1 teaspoon sugar, 2 teaspoons salt, 1 teaspoon freshly-ground pepper and 1 teaspoon Hungarian paprika in a salad bowl that has been rubbed with cut garlic. Mix well together.

Add 1 cup olive oil and 1/4 cup white wine vinegar and mix until dry ingredients are dissolved. Add a large ice cube, spear with a fork until the tines are imbedded in it and stir and stir until the ice is dissolved and the dressing is completely homogenized. Place salad greens into the dressing and stir until each bit is well-coated.

## Charlotte Russe

Soften 1 envelope plain gelatin in 1 cup milk in the top of a double boiler. Beat 4 egg yolks until lemon-colored, add 1/4 cup sugar and 1/4 teaspoon salt. Add to gelatin mixture and cook over simmering water, stirring until smooth. Add 1/4 teaspoon vanilla; allow to cool.

Beat 4 egg whites until soft peaks form and gradually beat in 1/4 cup sugar. Fold egg whites gently into cool custard. Blend in 1 tablespoon of sherry or Madeira.

Whip 1 cup heavy cream until stiff; fold into the custard mixture.

Line a glass bowl with split ladyfingers and sprinkle them with the same kind of wine you used in the custard. Pour the custard into the bowl and chill several hours or overnight. Decorate with additional whipped cream before serving.

## Pumpkin Pie

Line a 9-inch pan with pastry, crimping the edges high. Mix together: 1 tablespoon flour, 1/2 cup dark brown sugar, 1/2 teaspoon salt, 2 teaspoons cinnamon, 1/2 teaspoon ground ginger and 1/2 teaspoon ground nutmeg. Blend thoroughly into 1 1/2 cups of cooked, pureed pumpkin. Then beat in 1 cup heavy cream, 2 tablespoons molasses, 2 well-beaten eggs and 1/4 cup brandy.

Pour into the unbaked pie shell and bake 1 hour at 325 degrees, or until a knife inserted in center comes out dry. Cool and serve with wedges of cheddar cheese.

# Crowd-Pleaser Menu

Want a spectacular entrée for 24? This enormous chicken pie, baked in an eight-quart pan, is more than a conversation piece; it will astound you with its superb flavor. No casserole large enough for such a production? Try a small aluminum or enamel dishpan.

## Enormous Chicken Pie

*The pastry:*

    8 cups flour
    2 teaspoons salt
    2 cups butter
    2 cups vegetable shortening
    About 2 cups cold water
    An egg, beaten with a tablespoon cold water

Combine flour and salt. With fingers or pastry blender, work in the butter and shortening until mixture looks like coarse crumbs. Sprinkle with water, tossing with a fork, until mixture will form a firm dough. Chill well.

First, line a big, 8-quart pan: Roll out about 2/5 of the dough. (Measure the pan to be sure you roll a large enough circle to fit.) Reserve remaining dough for middle and top. It is somewhat difficult to handle a piece of pastry this large, but if (and when) it breaks, it can be mended by sticking patches of pastry in any holes, using water for "glue." Fit the dough loosely, without stretching, so it won't shrink, then trim off even with top edge of pan. Prick pastry thoroughly all over with a fork and it should not bubble or break in baking. Bake 15 minutes at 400 degrees and set aside.

*The filling:*

    (Use a very large, heavy kettle; there will be about 7
       quarts of filling.)
    3 1/2 quarts cubed cooked chicken (or use two 3-pound
       chickens and a small turkey breast)
    2 large onions, sliced
    1 cup butter
    1 1/2 cups flour
    3 quarts (12 cups) rich chicken broth (if there is not
       enough left from the simmering of the chicken,
       fill out with canned broth)
    1 cup light cream
    2 teaspoons white pepper
    Salt to taste
    A can (about 1/2 cup) pimiento, sliced
    1 cup currants, soaked 15 minutes in boiling water
    1 10 1/2-ounce package frozen peas, or use a No. 2
       can

Melt butter in large, heavy kettle and saute onion until transparent. Remove from heat and stir in flour. Slowly add chicken broth, stirring to keep it smooth. Replace on medium-high heat and cook, stirring, until thickened. Add cream, seasonings, pimiento, currants, chicken and peas and simmer slowly for ½ hour. Remove from heat and let stand while you roll pastry for middle crust.

Using slightly less than half the remaining pastry, roll a circle the size of your big pie pan, measured mid-way between top and bottom. Pour half the chicken filling into the pre-baked crust and cover with the circle of pastry. Bake 15 to 20 minutes at 400 degrees, until pastry is done but not necessarily brown.

Now add remaining filling and top with remaining pastry, rolled out to be about 1½ inches larger than top of pan. Fold and crimp edges. Cut slits in top for steam to escape. Scraps of pastry, rolled and cut as desired, may be used to decorate top. Now brush entire top with the beaten egg mixed with water. Bake about 45 minutes at 400 degrees, or until top is beautifully browned. Serves 24.

## Green Beans for a Bunch

    4 large (No. 2 1/2) cans Blue Lake-variety green beans
    1 envelope dry onion soup mix
    1/2 pound country ham scraps (substitute plain ham
       if necessary)

Place ingredients in a 4-quart pressure saucepan and cook under pressure for 30 minutes. Serves 12. To double recipe, borrow another pressure saucepan or pour out first batch of beans when they finish cooking, reserve them in a warm place and repeat the process.

## Fresh Herb and Kraut Relish for 24

    6 pounds sauerkraut
    3/4 cup chopped parsley
    1/4 cup fresh chives, chopped
    1 teaspoon dill seeds
    1 teaspoon savory
    3/4 cup mayonnaise

Drain sauerkraut and mix well with remaining ingredients. Chill several hours or overnight before serving. Serves 24.

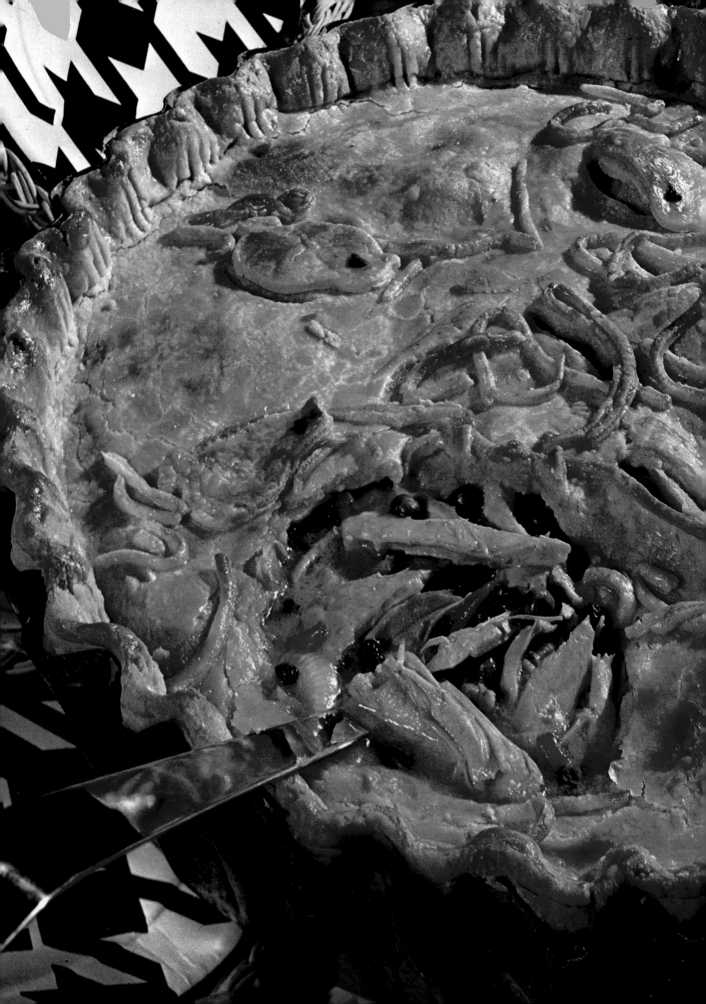

# Be Sure to Burgoo!

Somehow burgoo has become entwined in Kentucky Derby traditions, along with mint juleps and country ham. Yet Kentucky burgoo is good any time, especially in the fall. And contrary to what you may have heard, it doesn't have to be made outdoors in a big iron kettle over an open fire.

## Hart County Burgoo

2 pounds pork shank
2 pounds veal shank
2 pounds beef shank
2 pounds breast of lamb
A 4-pound hen
8 quarts water
1 1/2 pounds potatoes
1 1/2 pounds onions
1 bunch carrots
2 green peppers
2 cups chopped cabbage
1 quart tomato puree
2 cups whole corn, fresh or canned
2 pods red pepper
2 cups diced okra
2 cups lima beans
1 cup diced celery
Salt and cayenne to taste
Chopped parsley
Tabasco to taste
A-1 Sauce to taste
Worcestershire sauce to taste

Put all the meat into cold water and bring slowly to a boil. Simmer until it is tender enough to fall from the bones. Lift the meat out of the stock. Cool and chop up the meat, removing the bones.

Pare potatoes and onions. Dice. Return meat to stock and add potatoes and onions. Dice and add remaining vegetables. Allow to simmer along until thick. Burgoo should be very thick, but still "soupy." Season as it cooks, but not too much until almost done. Add chopped parsley just before the stew is ready to serve.

Stir frequently with a long-handled spoon or paddle during the first part of the cooking and almost constantly after it gets thick. Use at least a 4-gallon kettle and cook approximately 10 hours. Freezes well. Makes 12 quarts.

## Wayne County Burgoo

A 2 1/2-pound meaty shank of beef
A 3-pound chicken
Salt to taste
1 1/2 quarts canned or fresh tomatoes
1 cup diced celery
2 cups diced potatoes
2 cups diced carrots
2 cups fresh corn, cut from cob
1 cup cut green beans
1 cup peas (or a small can of peas)
1 package frozen lima beans
1 small can white soup beans
1/2 cup sliced okra
1 teaspoon pepper
1/4 teaspoon crushed red pepper (or more, to taste)
2 teaspoons sugar
1 can unseasoned chicken broth or water for thinning
1/2 cup flour, mixed with a cup of cream for thickening

The day before serving: brown beef in bacon fat. Add cold water to cover and add chicken and salt. Simmer, loosely covered, until meats are tender. Chicken will get done first; remove it and refrigerate, covered. Continue cooking beef until very tender, remove and refrigerate, covered. Strain broth and refrigerate.

The day of serving: Skim fat from broth. Remove chicken and beef from bones. Set aside. Measure the broth into a large kettle, at least 8-quart size, and add water to total 3 quarts. Add vegetables and seasonings and simmer, loosely covered, for at least 2 hours. The slower and longer the simmering, the better the burgoo. Stir often from the bottom. If it seems to be getting too thick, add water or chicken broth.

In the meantime, cut the meat in bite-size pieces and place in an oven-going container. Toss well to mix the meats and place in oven, covered, to be hot at serving time. The soup should be very thick, but still "soupy." If it seems thin, add the flour mixed with cream and cook, stirring until well thickened. Taste and correct seasonings.

To serve, place squares of egg cornbread in bottoms of large soup plates and ladle the soup onto the bread. Spoon the hot meat on top of each serving. This recipe makes 7 quarts. It will serve 12 to 15 generously and freezes very well.

In addition to the egg cornbread, a Wayne County burgoo dinner would include iced tea, lettuce-and-tomato salad and peach cobbler topped with vanilla ice cream.

# Currying Flavor

A spicy East Indian curry will wake up the most somnolent tastebuds. And doing a curry also qualifies as kitchen recreation—it's great sport to select and sample the condiments. The more condiments, the more fun it is. Dessert is fresh fruit and melon.

### Penang Prawn Curry (Shrimp)

1 tablespoon butter
1 onion, chopped fine
2 shallots, chopped (or use a little fresh, green onion, with a little of the tops)
1 clove garlic, crushed
About 4 stalks celery, with a few leaves, chopped
Sprigs of parsley, chopped
1 carrot, chopped
1 apple, chopped
1 green pepper, chopped
1 chili pepper (the red, hot kind)
1 bay leaf
1 pinch dried thyme
2 whole cloves
A few flakes dry mint
A little marjoram
1/4 teaspoon dried basil
2 tablespoons flour
1 quart hot water
1/2 teaspoon salt—or to taste
1/2 teaspoon pepper, or to taste
1/4 teaspoon cayenne pepper, or to taste
1/4 teaspoon nutmeg
1 ripe tomato, chopped
1 tablespoon curry powder
1 piece of lemon rind
2 cups prawns or shrimp shelled and cleaned
1 cup raw rice

Mix all ingredients with the exception of the shrimp and rice. Simmer for 1 hour. Strain into another saucepan. Add the prawns or shrimp and mix well. Simmer 10 minutes. Cook the rice with a little chopped parsley.

The rice may be served separately, with the curry alongside or in a platter or bowl with the shrimp curry on top. Or put the rice on a platter, make a well in the middle and pour the curry sauce into the well. Sprinkle all over with chopped parsley.

The recipe serves 4 to 6.

Any type meat or fish may be used instead of shrimp. All the seasonings can be adapted to taste. Curry is usually served with little side dishes. A typical Curry Condiment outlay includes chopped peanuts, chopped hard-cooked eggs, chopped green pepper, chutney (a must), crumbled Bombay duck (or crisp, crumbled cooked bacon), shredded fresh, canned or frozen-thawed coconut, chopped mustard pickle and soaked and drained raisins.

Each diner serves himself the curried shrimp and rice and then selects from the condiments to suit his appetite.

### Zucchini Casserole

Two 7- to 8-inch zucchinis
1 medium-sized onion, sliced
1 green pepper, sliced
3 good-sized ripe tomatoes

Cut the zucchini into rather thick slices, about ½ to ¾-inch thick. Do not peel, the skin is usually tender. Dip the slices of zucchini lightly in cracker meal, then in egg, diluted with 1 tablespoon of water or milk, and then in cracker crumbs once more. Sauté or fry in melted butter or margarine. Place in the bottom of a buttered 7-inch casserole. There should be enough for 2 or 3 layers of the sautéed zucchini.

Sauté onion, sliced green pepper, then add peeled tomato cut in slices or chunks. Season with salt and pepper and a little sugar—to taste.

Simmer until the tomatoes are tender. Then spread over the zucchini. Bake at 325 degrees about an hour. Top with buttered bread crumbs, put back into oven for 15 minutes, or until the crumbs are nicely browned.

### Deviled Bread Sticks

For a package of bread sticks, melt:

2/3 stick butter or margarine in a skillet, add:
2 cloves garlic chopped fine
3 tablespoons Worcestershire sauce
A scant teaspoon salt

Turn the heat low. Fill bottom of skillet with Italian bread sticks and turn them quickly so they will be coated with the mixture on all sides. After coating, stack them to make room for more. Sauté for 2 to 3 minutes, turning them constantly with a pancake turner or a spatula.

Transfer bread sticks to a cookie sheet, leaving space between them. Bake at about 250 degrees for 30 to 45 minutes until crisp and dry. Makes 24. Use with salads and soups, too.

# Spaghetti Sauces

A spaghetti dinner for eight on the agenda? Caruso Sauce—that's the one made with chicken livers—may be just what's called for to please chicken-liver lovers. For disdainers, make a delicious beef sauce. Serve a crisp green salad, crusty bread, and fruit and cheese for dessert.

## Italian Spaghetti with Caruso Sauce

    5 tablespoons salad oil or olive oil
    1/2 cup chopped onions
    1 large clove garlic, minced
    2-cans (1 pound 13 ounces each) Italian tomatoes
        (about 6 1/2 cups)
    2 cans (6 ounces each) tomato paste
    1 1/4 cups water
    1 1/2 tablespoons salt
    1/4 to 1/2 teaspoon pepper
    1 teaspoon oregano or sweet basil
    2 bay leaves
    1 tablespoon sugar
    1/4 cup grated Parmesan cheese
    1 pound chicken livers, cut in 1/2-inch pieces
    1 1/2 cups sliced mushrooms, drained
    1 teaspoon salt
    1 1/2 packages (1 1/2 pounds) uncooked spaghetti
    3 tablespoons butter

Heat 3 tablespoons of the oil in a heavy pot. Add onions and garlic and sauté until golden brown. Add tomatoes, breaking slightly with a fork. Add tomato paste, water, the salt, pepper, oregano, bay leaves, sugar and cheese. Mix well. Simmer over low heat for 1½ hours, stirring occasionally. Sauté chicken livers and mushrooms with 1 teaspoon salt in the remaining 2 tablespoons oil. Add to sauce and cook ½ hour longer.

Cook spaghetti as directed on the package. Drain. Add butter and mix, tossing the spaghetti lightly until the butter is melted. Serve with hot sauce and more Parmesan cheese if you like. Makes about 8 servings of spaghetti and sauce.

## Spaghetti with Meat Sauce

    2 tablespoons olive oil
    1 large onion, sliced
    1 handful of minced parsley
    1 small carrot diced
    1 clove garlic stuck with a toothpick so it can be
        retrieved later
    1 1/2 pounds chopped beef
    1 8-ounce can tomato sauce
    1 can hot water
    1/2 teaspoon oregano
    Salt and pepper to taste
    1/2 pound mushrooms
    Grated rind of 1/2 lemon
    2 pounds spaghetti (for 8 servings)
    Parmesan cheese

Heat the olive oil in a large frying pan. Add onion, carrot, garlic and parsley. Put in the meat. Stir the meat so it cooks evenly. Pour in the tomato sauce and half the can of hot water. Heat and then pour in the second half-can of the hot water. After the sauce has started to cook again, add the oregano, salt and pepper to taste. Cover and simmer over low fire for an hour, stirring frequently. Add the mushrooms which have been sautéed in butter for 10 minutes. Continue to simmer another hour. Add the grated rind of the lemon.

If you are making this ahead of time, store in the refrigerator and add lemon rind just before serving. If the sauce gets too thick, add more hot water. This should make enough sauce for 8 servings of spaghetti.

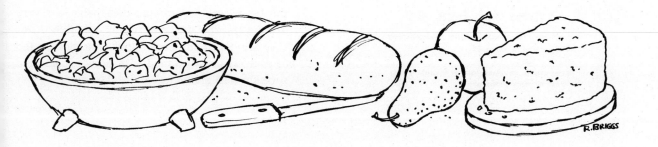

R. BRIGGS

# A Panful of Pollo

What better destiny for a three-pound chicken than to become the "Pollo" of Arroz con Pollo? Here are two versions of this popular dish, either of which will serve four most happily. Salad can be fruits or melon.

## Arroz con Pollo # 1

Oil for frying
1 chicken (3 pounds), cut in pieces
Salt and pepper
1 medium-sized onion, minced
1 mashed clove of garlic
1/2 cup tomato purée
3 cups chicken broth
1 cup raw rice
1/4 cup peas (optional)
1/2 teaspoon paprika
1 tablespoon chopped parsley
1 small can pimientos

Simmer the giblets and neck in water to make a broth. Adding a couple of wings and chicken stock heightens the flavor, and doesn't detract from the fresh flavor of the cooked giblets.

Brown the chicken in hot oil, seasoning it well with salt and pepper. Remove chicken and cook the onions until they have the "hue of daffodils," along with the garlic. This takes only a few minutes. Add tomato purée and broth. Return chicken to the cooking vessel and simmer 30 minutes. Add rice, peas (if you are using them) and paprika.

Cook uncovered about 30 minutes longer, or until all liquid is absorbed and rice and chicken are tender. The chopped parsley and sliced pimientos are added just before serving. This recipe is designed for 4 servings.

An electric skillet works wonderfully well. Use your own judgment as to the covering and uncovering after the rice is in. Don't stir with a spoon; if you feel you must stir use a fork.

## Arroz con Pollo # 2

A ready-to-cook chicken, about 3 pounds, cut up
1/4 cup salad or olive oil
1 cup raw rice
1 large onion, chopped (about 1 cup)
2 cloves of garlic, minced

2 cans (about 1 pound each) tomatoes
1 can (3 to 4 ounces) chopped mushrooms
1 can (about 4 ounces) pimientos, diced
2 tablespoons chopped parsley
1 1/2 teaspoon salt
1/8 teaspoon pepper

Brown the chicken on all sides in hot oil in a heavy frying pan. Drain on absorbent paper. Place in a 3-quart baking dish. Keep warm.

Sauté rice in the same frying pan, stirring often, about 5 minutes, or until golden brown. Add onion and garlic. Sauté over low heat for 10 minutes, or until just tender.

Stir in tomatoes, mushrooms, diced pimientos, parsley, salt and pepper. Bring to boiling, stirring often. Pour hot tomato mixture over chicken in casserole. Cover.

Bake in a moderate oven, 350 degrees, for 30 minutes. Uncover. Bake 40 minutes longer, or until rice and chicken are tender and the liquid is absorbed. 4 servings.

## Meringues with Sour Cream and Brown Sugar

3 egg whites
Pinch of cream of tartar
Pinch of salt
1 cup sugar
1 teaspoon lemon or vanilla extract

Beat the egg whites very stiff with the cream of tartar and salt, and beat in the sugar gradually, until the mixture stands in peaks. Add flavoring and drop by tablespoons onto well-buttered baking sheet. Wet the spoon and make a nest in the top of each meringue, then bake in a very slow oven, 250 degrees, for 30 minutes. After they are baked and cooled, put on a nice mound of sour cream sweetened with brown sugar, and sprinkle with grated nutmeg and cinnamon.

# Serving Sea Fare

Get some white fish, shrimp and lobster. Cook them with chopped vegetables in a rich broth of garlic-flavored clam juice. Then serve Bouillabaisse to the most deserving seafood enthusiasts on your list. They'll love you forever.

## Bouillabaisse for Eight

1/4 cup olive oil
2 cups clam juice
1 bay leaf
1/4 teaspoon thyme
1/4 teaspoon saffron (optional)
2 teaspoons salt
Pepper to taste
1 cup boiling water, maybe more
2 cloves garlic, minced
3 pounds prepared fish, cut in 3-inch pieces
1 pound or more shrimp and lobster tails
1 large onion, chopped
3 medium tomatoes, chopped
2 leeks, chopped (if not available, use another onion)
1 stalk celery, chopped
1 carrot, chopped
1 cup white wine (or substitute that much more clam juice)

Cook the chopped vegetables in the olive oil in a large kettle until they are done but not browned. Add the boiling water, clam juice and seasonings. Carefully lay the fish pieces on top of the cooked vegetables and boil hard with the lid on for 8 minutes. Then put the prepared shrimp and cracked lobster tails on top of the fish and boil hard again for 3 minutes.

The level of the liquid should be such that the pieces of fish show a little above the stock. If there isn't enough liquid, add some more clam juice or water. Add the wine, turn off the heat and let it set for a few minutes.

To serve, lay toasted slices of French bread in the bottom of a tureen and carefully ladle the stew on it. If making individual servings, put a slice of the toasted bread in the bottom of each bowl and add a generous helping of the bouillabaisse.

## Dependable French Bread

1 package or cake of yeast
2 cups warm water (85 degrees for yeast cake; 110 for granular yeast; if water is too hot, it will kill the yeast)
1 tablespoon sugar
2 teaspoons salt
5 to 6 cups flour
1 egg white, slightly beaten with 1 tablespoon water

Dissolve yeast in water. Add sugar, salt and about half the flour. Beat well with electric mixer. Then with a wooden spoon, stir in enough remaining flour to make a soft dough.

For kneading, use a clean, smooth tea towel, folded in half, with flour rubbed into it. Pick up its floured corners and, holding the cloth under the heel of your hand, push down the dough, which remains centered on the cloth. Turn the dough over once during the kneading process, and continue to knead until the dough is smooth and elastic—about 10 minutes. Use just enough flour to keep dough from sticking.

Cover the dough with a towel and let it rest for 20 minutes. Then cut the dough in half.

Roll one half at a time, into a long rectangle; then roll it up, starting with a long side. Seal the loose edge to the loaf. Put the loaves, seam downward, on cookie sheets greased and dusted with cornmeal. Cut diagonal slits ¼-inch deep and 3 inches apart. Brush loaves with the egg white and water mixture. Cover with greased wax paper. Refrigerate 4-24 hours. Preheat oven to 400 degrees before baking 30 to 35 minutes. Brush again with the egg-water and return to oven a couple of minutes.

# Turkey Hash Smash

If you want to carve your turkey with a spoon, first you must make a hash of it. Not just any hash, but Turkey Marguerite, with a rich and flavorful sauce, on a hearty foundation of noodles. A shapely mold of asparagus jellied in consommé madrilene complements the casserole.

### Turkey or Chicken Marguerite

    5 cups cooked, diced chicken or turkey

*Sauce:*

    9 tablespoons of butter or margarine
        (or strained turkey fat)
    9 tablespoons flour
    3 cups of rich milk (part cream is better)
    1 teaspoon salt
    1/8 teaspoon pepper or use Tabasco
    1/4 cup sherry wine or a little lemon juice
    1/2 to one cup chopped ripe olives (optional)

*The noodle part:*

    2 8-ounce packages green noodles
    Grated Swiss cheese

The sauce making comes first:

Melt the butter or margarine in a saucepan or the top of a double boiler. Blend in flour. Gradually add the milk, or milk and cream. Stir and cook slowly until thick and smooth. Season with the salt and pepper. Add sherry and taste. Then add olives, and let the sauce "stand by," until the noodles are cooked.

*Noodle Cooking*

Cook the noodles according to the directions on the package. The noodles may be broad, medium or small. Drain in a colander and pour about 2 cups of hot water over them. Drain again. Arrange the noodles in a flat baking dish. Pour a little of the sauce over the noodles. Mix the chicken with the rest of the sauce and spoon it over the noodles. Cover with grated cheese, and if the ingredients are still hot, keep under the broiler just long enough to brown the top. If you have prepared the dish earlier and refrigerated it, bake 20 minutes in a 375-degree oven and then brown in the broiler.

### Asparagus Mold

    1 package of frozen asparagus (or fresh in season)
    1/4 cup cold water
    1/2 tablespoon gelatin
    1 can of consommé madrilene
    1 tablespoon lemon juice
    1/2 teaspoon salt
    1/8 teaspoon black pepper (or cayenne,
        judging amount by taste)
    1 1/2 pint ring mold, wet with cold water

Cut up the cooked asparagus. Drain and cool. Sprinkle the gelatin in the cold water in a bowl and stir together. Heat the consommé, add lemon juice and seasonings, pour into the soaked gelatin, and stir until dissolved. Cool. Add the asparagus. Set aside until thick enough to keep asparagus from settling in the bottom, stirring occasionally. Turn into the mold and chill for 5 to 6 hours. Unmold and serve with sour cream-mayonnaise (recipe below). **6** servings.

*Sour Cream-Mayonnaise Dressing*

    1/2 cup mayonnaise
    1/2 cup sour cream
    1 tablespoon tomato catsup
    1 teaspoon lemon juice

Mix all ingredients together to chill. The catsup may be omitted, and if you omitted them in the Marguerite, chop and add about 6 large ripe olives.

### Bimini Parfait

Fill dessert glass about one third with vanilla ice cream. Add a layer of coffee caramel sauce, then a layer of fudge sauce (recipes follow). Fill with ice cream. Add more fudge sauce. Top with whipped cream dusted with instant coffee.

*Coffee Caramel Sauce*

    3/4 cup brown sugar, firmly packed
    1 cup sugar, granulated
    2/3 cup light corn syrup
    1/4 cup butter or margarine
    A pinch of salt
    1/3 cup cream
    1/2 teaspoon vanilla
    1/2 cup strong coffee

Combine the two sugars, corn syrup, butter and salt in a saucepan. Cook, stirring, until sugar dissolves. Cook without stirring to 236 degrees on a candy thermometer or to the soft-ball stage. Cool slightly. Stir in cream, vanilla and coffee. Makes about 2 cups.

*Fudge Sauce*

    4 squares unsweetened chocolate
    1 cup sugar
    2 tablespoons butter or margarine
    2 small cans (1 1/2 cups) evaporated milk
    2 teaspoons vanilla

Melt chocolate over hot water. Stir in sugar gradually. Add butter, stir until melted. Stir in evaporated milk slowly. Cook over hot water, stirring often, until thickened. Add vanilla and cool. Makes 2 cups.

# Soup 'n' Sandwich

For fullest effect, lentil soup should be eaten on a cold, cold night. And to complement the soup, serve the king of sandwiches: the Reuben. Men find it irresistible, combining the trusted corned beef, Swiss cheese and pumpernickel with nippy sauerkraut, all grilled and very rich.

## Lentil Soup

Ham bone with at least a pound of meat adhering to it (the end of a cooked ham)
1-pound package lentils
3 carrots, chopped
1 large onion, chopped
4 stalks celery, chopped
Salt and pepper
Water or bouillon to thin soup, if necessary

Soak the lentils in 2 cups water for an hour, while the ham bone simmers in a quart of water. Remove the meat from the bone and return meat to the kettle, along with the lentils (soaking water and all) and the chopped vegetables. Simmer, stirring frequently, for an hour. Season to taste with salt and pepper. If it gets too thick, add water or bouillon.

## Reuben Sandwiches

You'll need cooked corned beef, sliced paper-thin, Swiss cheese, dark rye or pumpernickel bread, sauerkraut, good mayonnaise and butter.

Spread bread slices lightly with mayonnaise. On one slice, arrange several slivers of corned beef. On the other slice of bread place a generous slice of Swiss cheese. Drain sauerkraut well. Cover beef or cheese with kraut, sandwiching it between.

Butter both outside pieces and grill slowly until the cheese melts. The sandwiches should be weighted; best is a grill with its own fitted cover. Serve the sandwiches immediately, with hot mustard and a relish tray.

# Veal Breast Fest

Breast of veal prepared with a luscious stuffing makes a delicious and relatively inexpensive basis for this menu. Beet Velvet Salad with cucumbers is just one of the enchantments along the way to Chocolate Chip Tortoni, a heavenly dessert.

## Stuffed Veal Breast

3-pound veal breast (have butcher cut pocket)
1/2 cup butter or margarine
1/2 cup onions, sliced thin
1/2 cup celery, cut fine
1/4 cup green pepper, chopped fine
6 slices of toasted bread
1 teaspoon salt
1/4 teaspoon pepper
1/2 teaspoon sage
1 whole egg
1/4 cup chopped pimiento
1 small clove garlic, halved and stuck on toothpicks

Melt butter or margarine and add onions. Sauté the onions along with the celery, green pepper and garlic. Remove garlic. Cover and simmer until vegetables are tender, about 15 minutes. Pour over toasted bread that has been soaked in water and pressed dry. Add egg and mix with two forks to keep it light, adding, as you mix, the salt, pepper, sage and pimiento.

Sponge the veal and pat dry with paper towels. Fill the pocket the butcher has cut with the dressing, then skewer or sew together.

Place on rack in a roasting pan and roast in a preheated 325-degree oven for about 2½ hours, or until the breast is fork-tender. Roast with breast side up the first hour, breast side down the second hour, and breast side up the last half hour.

Baste roast every half hour with tomato juice or a mixture of 1 tablespoon butter or margarine, a tablespoon tomato paste and ½ cup water. Add 1 cup water to the roasting pan, after the first half hour of cooking, for gravy liquid later.

At the end of roasting time, thicken the juices with a little flour or cornstarch and water, then season according to taste.

Approximately 6 portions.

Serve on a platter surrounded by baked apple halves topped with apricots.

Core, pare and cut 6 apples in halves. Mix a cup of sugar with a cup of water and boil, stirring until sugar is dissolved, about 5 minutes. Add the juice of ½ lemon. Place apples in baking dish and pour this sauce over them. Cover and bake in a moderate oven (375 degrees) until apples are tender (about 30 minutes). Baste frequently with the syrup in baking dish. Remove carefully to the serving platter and top each half with a canned apricot.

## Baked Sweet Potatoes and Oranges

3 large sweet potatoes
2 medium-size oranges
1/2 cup boiling water
1/3 cup brown sugar, firmly packed
1 teaspoon salt
3 tablespoons melted butter
1/2 cup crushed corn flakes or chopped pecans

Cook sweet potatoes in their scrubbed jackets until they are just tender. Combine sugar, water, salt and butter and cook until slightly thickened. Drain and peel the sweet potatoes and cut into ½-inch slices. Peel the oranges, removing all the white membranes and cut them into ½-inch slices.

In a buttered baking dish alternate layers of sliced sweet potatoes and oranges. Pour syrup over all. Sprinkle with crushed corn flakes or pecans and bake in a 350-degree oven for about 30 minutes.

## Browned Turnips

8 turnips
3 to 4 tablespoons butter or other fat
2 to 3 or more tablespoons brown sugar
Canned bouillon or bouillon cube and water
Salt to taste

Peel and cube turnips. Boil until tender in bouillon. It takes very little cooking to make them tender; don't overcook. Heat fat in skillet. Add parboiled cubes of turnips and sprinkle them with brown sugar. Turn and brown the turnips. To keep warm, add a couple of tablespoons water and cover until serving time.

## Spinach Supreme

3 pounds spinach (or 3 packages frozen spinach)
1/2 cup sauterne
2 tablespoons butter or margarine
1/4 cups flour
1 cup milk
1 teaspoon sugar
Salt, pepper, curry powder to taste

Clean the spinach and cook in the sauterne 12 to 15 minutes. Cool completely. Press through a food chopper or chop very fine. Make a cream sauce by melting the butter, adding flour and blending until smooth, heating thoroughly. Gradually add milk and about 1 cup of the juice off the spinach. Add chopped spinach. Season with salt, pepper, the teaspoon of sugar, and the curry.

*Continued*

103

## Beet Velvet

1 package lemon-flavored gelatin
1 cup hot water
2 (4 1/2-ounce) cans strained baby food beets
1/2 pint dairy sour cream
1 tablespoon lemon juice
1 teaspoon grated onion
Salt and pepper
1/8 teaspoon monosodium glutamate

Dissolve gelatin in hot water. Let cool a little and then blend in all the other ingredients. Pour into individual molds or one large mold. Serve with mayonnaise. 6 servings.

## Crusty Onion Popovers

1 cup milk
1/2 teaspoon salt
1 tablespoon melted butter
3 eggs, well beaten
1 cup sifted flour
1/2 teaspoon onion salt
1/4 cup grated onion

Brush 6 baking cups or popover pans with cooking oil. Combine milk, salt, butter and eggs. Add flour and onion salt and beat until smooth. Add grated onion. Blend in. Fill cups 2/3 full. Bake 400 degrees, 45-50 minutes.

## Chocolate Chip Tortoni

2 eggs
2 teaspoons cornstarch
2 tablespoons sugar
1 cup milk
1 teaspoon vanilla
2 tablespoons rum or 1 teaspoon rum extract, or to taste
1 square (1 ounce) unsweetened chocolate
3 tablespoons (1 ounce) candied fruit
6 macaroons
1/2 pint heavy whipping cream, whipped

Separate eggs, putting the yolks in a heavy saucepan or the top of a double boiler. Mix egg yolks, sugar and all but about ¼ cup of milk together. Mix the ¼ cup of milk gradually with the cornstarch and add it to the egg yolk mixture. Blend all together thoroughly and cook gently over boiling water, until it is smooth. Cool. Add flavoring. Grate chocolate very fine, and add along with the finely chopped fruit. Break macaroons in little pieces and stir them with the candied fruit and chocolate into the custard mixture. Fold in whipped cream. Beat the egg whites and fold them gently.

Pile into custard cups or into a freezing tray for 2 to 3 hours.

R. BRIGGS

# A Gastronomic Tour

Without leaving home except for a brief sortie to the supermarket, you can take a gastronomic tour of Europe: This worldly composite of foods will whisk your dinner guests all the way from Spain to Scotland, with a couple of delectable stopovers along the way.

## Mandelmilchsuppe

2 cups ground blanched almonds
1/2 cup butter
2 quarts milk
6 chicken bouillon cubes
4 teaspoons cornstarch
2 teaspoons monosodium glutamate
1/2 teaspoon sugar
For garnish, toasted slivered almonds

Sauté ground almonds in butter until lightly browned. Stir in milk. Crush bouillon cubes and mix with the cornstarch, sugar and mono-sodium glutamate. Stir into almond mixture. Simmer, stirring frequently, until slightly thickened. To serve, ladle into soup plates or bowls and garnish with toasted, slivered almonds. Serves 8 or more.

## Souvlakia (Shish Kebob)

1/2 pound tender lean beef per person, cut in 1-inch cubes (or use lamb)
1 cup olive oil
1/2 cup lemon juice
1 cup dry white wine
2 teaspoons salt
1/2 teaspoon pepper
1/2 teaspoon oregano
2 cloves garlic, minced
2 bay leaves

Combine all ingredients except meat to make a marinade. Add cubed meat and allow to stand overnight in refrigerator, or for at least 6 hours. Drain meat well and thread on skewers alternately with:

Small white onions, peeled and boiled almost tender
Bite-size squares of green pepper
Red cherry tomatoes
Pineapple chunks
Fresh mushrooms

After grilling over hot charcoal for 10 to 15 minutes they'll be ready to serve with brown rice, made as follows:

2 cups natural brown rice
5 cups water (use half chicken broth for tastier rice)
2 teaspoons salt
2 tablespoons butter
1/2 cup pine nuts
1/2 cup chopped black olives

Place rice, water or broth, salt and butter in large saucepan. Bring to boiling, lower heat, cover and allow to simmer for 50 minutes. Stir in pine nuts and chopped black olives. Serves 8-12.

## Esparragos con Salsa de Anchos

2 10-ounce packages frozen asparagus
1/2 cup salad oil
3 tablespoons lemon juice
1 tablespoon anchovy paste
1 tablespoon onion juice
1 teaspoon chervil
1 small clove garlic, minced

Combine all ingredients except asparagus. Thaw asparagus and lay the spears in a deep bowl. Pour marinade over and refrigerate 6 hours or overnight. At serving time, drain asparagus and arrange over crisp lettuce leaves. Serves 8.

## Scottish Border Tart

1 cup flour
1/4 teaspoon salt
1 tablespoon sugar
1/3 cup butter
1 egg yolk
1 tablespoon water

Sift flour, salt and sugar into a bowl. Cut in butter with a pastry blender until mixure is mealy looking. Add water to the egg yolk and stir into the flour mixture with a fork. Work with the hands until dough is pliable. Roll out quickly on a lightly floured piece of waxed paper to help transfer the crust to an 8-inch pie plate or flan tin. Add the filling.

1/4 cup margarine
3 tablespoons sugar
1 egg
1/2 teaspoon vanilla
1 cup fruit (raisins, chopped glacé, cherries and currants, combined)

Cream margarine and sugar until light and fluffy. Beat in the egg, fruit and vanilla. Pour in lined pie plate. Bake in moderate oven (350 degrees) 20 to 30 minutes.

Drizzle vanilla frosting with a drop of lemon extract added over the top. About 8 small but rich servings.

# Mmm... Meat Loaf!

Begin dinner with Shrimp Rémoulade and end it with cheesecake and nobody will care much what is served in between. But if there is a great meat loaf and a fascinating vegetable to bridge the gap, so much the better!

### Louisiana Shrimp Rémoulade

1 pound shrimp
Vinegar
4 tablespoons olive oil
2 tablespoons dried tarragon
1 teaspoon salt, or to taste
2 tablespoons creole mustard
2 tablespoons anchovy paste
1/2 teaspoon paprika
4 stalks celery (chopped fine)
4 small onions (chopped fine)
bay leaves
4 sprigs parsley
Red pepper, to taste
Horseradish, to taste

Boil shrimp, seasoned in water with red pepper, salt, onions, bay leaves (and you might add a little onion juice or vinegar). When shrimp is cooked, peel and vein it. Make dressing of the oil, vinegar and salt. Add remaining ingredients and mix well. (If it's too thick, add more oil and vinegar.) Pour over shrimp. Let stand 24 hours in refrigerator to marinate well. Serve on shredded lettuce.

### Famous Meat Loaf

1 cup milk
2/3 cup dry bread crumbs
1 1/2 pounds ground round
2 slightly beaten eggs
1/4 cup chopped onion, or onion powder used discreetly
1 teaspoon salt
1/8 teaspoon pepper
1 teaspoon sugar
1 teaspoon prepared mustard
1 teaspoon horseradish
Catsup to taste
Bacon strips

Scald the milk and add the bread crumbs. Let stand. Mix together all the other ingredients. Add milk and bread crumbs. Form into a loaf. Pour a little more catsup over the top of the loaf, add strips of bacon, and bake in a 350-degree oven for 1 hour. When finished, top with sautéed mushrooms.

To the platter, add Brussels sprouts, cooked just freshly tender, and still a delightful green, seasoned with salt, pepper, melted butter and lemon juice.

On the other side of the platter, use fresh, young potatoes. They should be tender, but firm. Dry them off after boiling by pouring off any excess water and by shaking the saucepan over a low flame. Then roll them in seasoned butter and chopped parsley.

### Scalloped Salsify Casserole

3 1/2 cups cooked salsify
3/4 cup chopped celery
Chopped green pepper, or canned pimiento
1 cup white sauce
1/2 cup dry bread crumbs
3 tablespoons butter

Wash and pare the salsify. Put pared roots into slightly acidulated water to prevent darkening. Cut roots 1-inch lengths. Cook in boiling water until tender.

Place alternate layers of salsify and celery, along with the green pepper, or pimiento in greased baking dish. Add seasoned white sauce. Cover with bread crumbs and dot with butter. Place in moderate oven, 375 degrees for about 25 minutes.

### Hammack-Kilgus Cheesecake

1 1/2 cups zwieback crumbs (one 5 1/2-ounce box)
2 tablespoons butter or margarine
2 tablespoons sugar

Blend crumbs with butter and sugar. Spread on the bottom and sides of a greased 9-inch spring mold. Save a few crumbs back to decorate the top.

*Filling*

2 8-ounce packages cream cheese
1 cup sugar
5 egg yolks
1 pint sour cream
1 teaspoon vanilla
2 teaspoons lemon juice
5 egg whites, beaten stiffly

Cream cheese in a large bowl. Add sugar, beating, and the unbeaten egg yolks. Stir just enough to blend the egg yolks. Add sour cream, vanilla and lemon juice. Fold in egg whites.

Pour mixture into the crumb crust. Sprinkle the saved crumbs on top. Bake in 300-degree oven 1 hour. Turn off heat; let cake stand in oven for 1 more hour with the door closed. Then open oven door and let it stand another ½ hour. Refrigerate overnight.

# Career-Girl Cuisine

When the "working girl" cooks for herself, that's one thing. But when she entertains, dinner must be special. That's easier said than done, when it's likely she gets home only an hour before her guests arrive. Boeuf Bourguignon can be prepared the night before, which gives quite a "leg up" on the fixings.

### Boeuf Bourguignon for Four

3 tablespoons margarine (or 1 1/2 tablespoons each margarine and oil)
2 pounds beef chuck or stew beef, cut in inch cubes
1 small clove garlic, minced
3 small onions, sliced
3 tablespoons flour
1 cup dry Burgundy wine
1/2 cup water
1 1/4 teaspoons salt
1/2 teaspoon monosodium glutamate
1/4 teaspoon pepper
1/4 teaspoon marjoram
1/4 teaspoon oregano
1/2 cup strong black coffee
1/2 teaspoon bottled brown gravy coloring

Heat margarine and oil in deep frying pan and brown meat on all sides. Add garlic and onions and cook until onions are soft but not brown. Remove meat and onions from pan.

Blend flour with remaining oil in pan. Gradually add wine, water, seasonings, brown gravy coloring and coffee. Stir until slightly thickened. Return meat and onions to pan and cover. Simmer 1½ hours, or until meat is tender. If prepared for serving next day, cool quickly and refrigerate. At serving time, just bring it to a boil again and let simmer while preparing the noodles.

### Platter of Noodles and Brussels Sprouts

1 8-ounce package narrow noodles, or 4 ounces each narrow white noodles and green spinach noodles
Salt and pepper to taste
1 10-ounce package frozen Brussels sprouts
4 tablespoons butter

Bring 3 quarts of water to boil in large kettle, add about a tablespoon salt and drop in the noodles. (If you decide on both green and white noodles for color interest, use 2 pots of salted water and cook them separately.) Boil noodles 13 to 15 minutes, or until tender. Drain and stir 3 tablespoons butter into noodles.

Cook Brussels sprouts according to package directions, drain and season with remaining tablespoon butter. Arrange noodles on a well-heated platter and place the Brussels sprouts around edges. Ladle the hot Bourguignon into center of noodles. Use warmed dinner plates. It serves 4.

### Blue Cheese-Celery Seed Dressing

1 cup sour cream
2 tablespoons vinegar
1 teaspoon sugar
1 teaspoon salt
1/4 teaspoon dry mustard
1/2 teaspoon celery seed
1/4 cup blue cheese (about 1 1/4 ounces)
Dash pepper
Dash paprika for garnish

Combine all ingredients and store in refrigerator until serving time. (It keeps well.) Stir and spoon over lettuce wedges or tossed salad. Sprinkle with paprika. Triple the sugar called for in the recipe for a good dressing over fruit salads.

### Chocolate Fondue

A 6-ounce package semisweet chocolate bits
1/3 cup shortening (or 1/2 shortening, 1/2 margarine)
3 cups assorted canned fruits and maraschino cherries

Cut the drained fruits (apricots, pears, peaches, pineapple chunks, whatever you choose) into bite-sized pieces. Place on a cookie sheet or other pan which has been covered with waxed paper. Insert a wooden pick in each bit and place in freezer.

Place chocolate bits in top of double broiler and add shortening. Heat, stirring, over hot but not boiling water, until melted. To serve, pour chocolate in a miniature chafing dish over low heat and arrange the frozen fruit on a tray alongside. Guests dip fruit bits into chocolate, which hardens quickly around the cold fruit.

# How Sweet It Is!

Here is a trio of toothsome sweets for reference next time you issue a come-for-dessert invitation: Light as air, Apricot Charlotte Russe will serve eight divinely; to entertain a baker's dozen, a spectacular banana cake; if the number of "desserters" should run upwards of 30, make it Stack Pie, an old-fashioned conversation starter.

## Apricot Charlotte Russe

1 envelope plain gelatin
1/4 cup cold water
1/2 cup boiling water
1/4 cup sugar
Juice of 1/2 lemon
1 1/4 cups apricot preserves
1 cup heavy cream, whipped
Ladyfingers to line bowl
2 tablespoons apricot liqueur (or substitute orange juice)

Soften gelatin in cold water and pour boiling water over it. Stir to dissolve thoroughly. Add sugar, lemon juice and apricot preserves. Strain, using a wooden spoon to stir liquid, leaving the residue of the preserves in the strainer.

Refrigerate, or set the bowl in a larger bowl filled with ice and water and stir, until the consistency is of thick egg white. Fold in the stiffly beaten cream. Line a glass serving dish with laydfinger halves and sprinkle them with apricot liqueur. Turn charlotte mixture into the lined bowl. Chill several hours or overnight. Garnish with additional whipped cream if desired. 6 to 8 servings.

## Banana Delight Cake

2 1/2 cups sifted cake flour
1 2/3 cups sugar
1 1/4 teaspoons baking powder
1 1/4 teaspoons soda
1 teaspoon salt
2/3 cup vegetable shortening
2/3 cup buttermilk
1 1/4 cups mashed ripe bananas
2 eggs

Sift dry ingredients into large mixing bowl. Add shortening, buttermilk and bananas. Mix until all dry ingredients are dampened, then beat at low speed for 2 minutes. Add eggs and beat 1 minute. Grease two 9-inch layer-cake pans and line with waxed paper. Divide batter

and bake at 350 degrees for 25 to 30 minutes. Remove from oven and let cool 5 minutes in the pans before removing to racks. Cool and frost.

## Banana-Nut Frosting

1/3 cup butter or margarine
2 pounds powdered sugar, sifted
1/2 cup mashed bananas
1 teaspoon lemon juice
1 cup toasted coconut
2/3 cup finely chopped nuts
4 drops yellow food coloring

Cream butter and add sugar and bananas, which have been sprinkled with lemon juice, and blend well. Add coconut and nuts, mix, then blend in yellow food coloring. Spread between layers and on sides of cake.

## Transparent Pies in a Stack

9 eggs, separated
3 cups white sugar
2 cups butter
1 cup light-brown sugar
1 pint cream
1 pint currant jelly
4 teaspoons vanilla
5 unbaked 9-inch pie shells with flat, not fluted, rims

Cream white sugar with the butter until light, then add yolks of eggs. Beat in cream, jelly and vanilla. Whip the egg whites and gradually add brown sugar to make a meringue. Fold meringue into the creamed mixture. Pour equal amounts into each of the 5 unbaked shells. Bake 10 minutes at 425, then at 350 degrees for about 30 minutes, or until filling is set. Filling in each pie should be rather thin. Don't stack them until an hour or so before serving, as the fillings could soak into the crust above. After stacking, dredge top pie, if desired, with sifted powdered sugar. About 25 to 30 servings.

# Lamb for Brunch

Start this hearty brunch with grapefruit halves garnished with grapes and laced with grenadine. Follow with broiled lamb chops, glorified or marinated, as you prefer. Lamb fries are on the menu, too, and they're a delicacy so neglected that few cookbooks mention them.

### Glorified Lamb Chops

6 thick lamb chops
1 teaspoon mustard
2 teaspoons butter or margarine
2 cups cracker crumbs
2 teaspoons salt
1/8 teaspoon pepper

Mix mustard and butter or margarine until well blended and spread over each lamb chop. Roll the chops in buttered cracker crumbs, season with salt and pepper, and broil until tender. 6 servings.

### Marinated Lamb Chops

4 thick kidney lamb chops
4 tablespoons olive oil
1 tablespoon tarragon vinegar
1 small onion, sliced thin
1 clove garlic, mashed
1 teaspoon salt
1/2 teaspoon coarsely ground black pepper
1 bay leaf, broken
A few sprigs parsley
A few strips lemon peel

Mix marinade ingredients well. Pour over chops. Put in refrigerator to soak for several hours before broiling. Turn occasionally. Broil.

### Lamb Fries

Lamb fries may be bought fresh or frozen. Fresh ones must be skinned if the butcher hasn't done it. The frozen ones sometimes come skinned and sliced. Whichever you use, soak them in salt water for about 20 minutes, before coating and frying. Dry well.

Roll in flour, then in egg which has been diluted with a tablespoon of water per egg used. Roll for the second time in seasoned flour. Fry gently in fat, as you would sweetbreads, until crusty and golden. Lift out. Drain and serve.

### Grits Soufflé with Shrimp or Ham

1 cup quick-cooking grits
4 cups boiling water
1 teaspoon salt
2 egg yolks
1 cup grated cheese
1 tablespoon butter
1 cup milk
1 cup cleaned shrimp (or ham)
Salt to taste
Tabasco to taste
2 egg whites, beaten stiff

Slowly add the grits to the salted, boiling water. Cook over direct heat for 2½ to 5 minutes, stirring occasionally.

Remove from heat when grits are well cooked. Add the egg yolks and grated cheese. Stir and fold in until cheese is melted. Add butter to hot mixture, milk, and the shrimp or ham. Season to taste with salt and Tabasco. Fold beaten egg whites into the grits mixture. Pour all into greased casserole and bake at about 325 degrees for 20 minutes, or until set. It should not be dry, nor too soft—but just right to be spooned in the same manner as you would spoon bread.

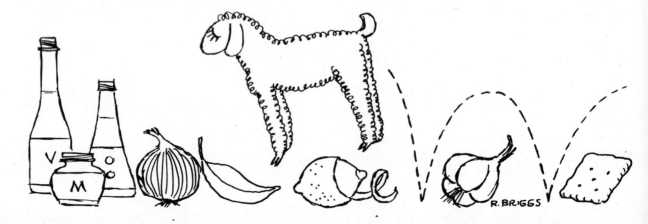

R. BRIGGS

# Tuna Fish Dish

Call it "Margaret's Really Good Tuna Dish," or slur it with a Southern accent so it becomes "Margarella, a good tuna dish." This one has been one of Cissy Gregg's most popular recipes over the years.

### Margarella

6 medium-sized onions, chopped
2 green peppers, diced
1/2 pound mushrooms, sliced
6 tablespoons butter or margarine
A small can of pimientos, chopped
2 cans (10 1/2-ounce) tomato soup
1/2 pint coffee cream
2 sweet red peppers, cut in strips (optional)
1/2 cup chutney
2 cans tuna fish
Salt and pepper to taste

Melt the butter or margarine in a skillet and add onions, green peppers, red peppers, if you are using them, pimientos and mushrooms. Cook and stir until the onions become transparent. Mix the tomato soup and cream together and stir them into the onion mixture. Bring to a boil and cook at moderate heat, a few minutes. Drain tuna. Break into bite-size chunks and add. Add the chutney last. Taste to correct seasonings. Stir well to blend.

Good served over wild rice or fried noodles.

### Almond Meringue Layer Torte

1/2 cup butter
1 cup powdered sugar, sifted
4 egg yolks, well beaten
1 cup sifted flour
1 teaspoon baking powder
1/4 teaspoon salt
3 tablespoons milk
1/2 teaspoon each almond extract and vanilla extract
4 egg whites
1 cup granulated sugar sifted with pinch of salt
Pinch of powdered ginger (optional)
1 cup blanched, toasted almonds, finely shredded

Cream butter until it is lemon-colored and fluffy. Add sifted powdered sugar and beat and cream until mixture is smooth. Add the well-beaten egg yolks and blend thoroughly. Sift flour; sift again with baking powder and salt. Blend the flour mixture into the butter-sugar mixture. Combine the 3 tablespoons of milk with the extracts and then add to mixture. Blend well. Pour batter into two 8-inch buttered and floured layer-cake pans. (Use either the slip-bottom or spring-form type.)

Beat egg whites until stiff, and gradually add to it the granulated sugar sifted with pinch of salt, and the ginger—blending constantly.

Dip a spatula in cold water and use to spread the beaten egg white-mixture over cake batter. Sprinkle tops generously with shredded almonds. Bake in slow oven, 300 degrees, for 50 to 60 minutes. Remove layers from pans and let cool. Spread one layer with Orange Cream Filling (recipe follows) and place other layer on top.

### Orange Cream Filling

1/3 cup flour, sifted
5/8 cup (10 tablespoons) granulated sugar
Pinch of salt
1 2/3 cups scalded milk
2 egg yolks, beaten
Rind from large orange, grated
1 tablespoon orange juice
1 teaspoon lemon juice

Sift and mix flour, sugar and salt. Place in top of double boiler. Slowly add scalded milk and stir until consistency is smooth. Then place the top of boiler directly over medium heat and cook, stirring constantly and vigorously, until thickened.

Beat egg yolks and add some of the milk mixture to them, stirring as you do. Pour this into the other mixture in the top of double boiler, which has been placed again over hot water. When thickened once more, remove instantly from double boiler, cool slightly, and add grated orange rind, orange juice and lemon juice. Set the pan in cold water until the mixture is lukewarm and begins to stiffen. Then spread the filling between layers of cake.

# A Roman Feast

One of the crowning glories of Italian cookery is veal with tuna gravy . . . . Vitello Tonnato. It is equally delicious served hot or cold; just make sure all the components (veal, rice and sauce) are all hot or all cold. Dessert is Strufoli, from Southern Italy.

## Vitello Tonnato

A 4-pound, boned and rolled veal rump roast
1/4 cup olive oil
1 large onion, chopped
1 rib celery, chopped
2 carrots, chopped
1 clove garlic, minced
1 2-ounce can anchovies, chopped
1 7 1/2-ounce can tuna
2 cups dry white wine (vermouth is good)
1 cup chicken broth, your own or canned
1 sour pickle, optional but good
1/2 teaspoon peppercorns (no salt needed)
1 bay leaf
Few sprigs parsley or 1 tablespoon dried parsley
1 tablespoon drained capers
1 teaspoon lemon juice
1 cup mayonnaise

Heat the olive oil in a large, heavy kettle and lightly brown the veal roast in it. Add all remaining ingredients except the capers, mayonnaise and lemon juice. Cover tightly and simmer gently until the meat is fork-tender, 1½ to 2 hours, turning or basting it occasionally in the liquid. Cool the veal in the broth, if it is to be served cold, and refrigerate. If you serve it hot, remove from the hot broth and keep in warm place while you make the sauce.

*Sauce:* Place the kettle containing all the ingredients (except meat, of course) over high heat and boil until liquid is reduced to about 1 cup. It will be very rich and concentrated. Strain. Mix the strained liquid with the cup of mayonnaise. Add capers and lemon juice.

*To Serve:* Prepare the rice according to package directions, allowing 1 cup cooked rice per person. Arrange on platter. Slice the veal and arrange on rice. Spoon some of the sauce over the meat and serve the remainder in a sauce boat. Keep everything (rice, veal and sauce) hot or everything cold.

## Strufoli (Honey Bubbles)

2 eggs
3 tablespoons butter, melted (or cooking oil)
1/4 teaspoon salt
1 teaspoon vanilla
1 3/4 cups flour
Oil for frying, 1-inch deep
1/2 cup sugar
1/2 cup honey
3 tablespoons candied cherries, cut up
3 tablespoons pine nuts (optional, but good)
Colored candy sprinkles

Beat the eggs with the butter, salt and vanilla. Add enough flour to make a soft manageable dough. Knead 5 minutes on floured dough board or cloth. Wrap in waxed paper and let stand for ½ hour. Roll dough ¼-inch thick. Cut the dough into tiny ¼-inch cubes: The simplest method is to cut the dough into quarters with a large knife and stack the pieces. Then slice ¼-inch wide down through the layers. Turn and cut these strips into ¼-inch bits. Spread the pieces and let them stand ½ hour.

Heat cooking oil to 375 degrees and fry a handful of the little dough bits at a time until they all are lightly browned. Drain on paper towels.

Heat the sugar with the honey in a heavy skillet until completely melted. Toss in the fried pastry all at one time, along with the chopped cherries and the pine nuts (if used) stirring with a wooden spoon to coat each morsel. Remove from skillet quickly and mound on buttered plate or waxed paper. Make just one mound, or pile into 6 individual mounds. The latter makes Strufoli easier to serve. Sprinkle with the colored candies. Six servings.

Strufoli will stay crisp and fresh several days covered with waxed paper at room temperature.

# Sourdough Knowhow

Sourdough baking, done with no yeast except the wild airborne kind, ties in with the resurgence of interest in home baking in general, a phenomenon probably traceable to the "plastic" tendency in modern foods. Make a sourdough starter and taste "real" bread again.

## Sourdough Starter

2 cups whole milk
2 cups flour

First, put the milk in a glass jar or crock and leave it, covered with a cloth, in a warm place (80 to 85 degrees) for about 24 hours, or until it sours. Stir in the flour and let stand again, lightly covered, at the same warm temperature, until bubbly and sour. It will take from 2 to 5 days. If a bit of black mold forms on the inside of the container, just wipe it away. It should have a good, healthy, yeasty, sour smell. If the sour odor is repugnant, it isn't right. It may be necessary to throw the mixture out and start over; it doesn't always work the first time.

Maintain about 3 cups of starter, as most recipes call for 1 or 2 cups. Replenish starter pot after each use. Immediately after measuring out the amount for the recipe, stir back into the pot enough milk and flour to bring the level up to the original amount Never, never put anything in the starter pot except the same 2 ingredients you started with. Leftover bits of dough will ruin it. After replenishing, leave the pot out of the refrigerator for a few hours until it starts bubbling again. Then refrigerate, covered but not sealed.

The starter should be used and replenished every 2 to 4 weeks. If a little clear liquid forms on top of the starter after standing for a long time, just stir it back in. It is an alcoholic liquid called "hootch" and it belongs there.

In sourdough baking, soda is used to counteract the sourness. Use the amount called for in each recipe to start, then increase it next time if the product seems too sour.

For storing the sourdough starter, a glass or glazed pottery container is best and should not be filled more than half full, as the mixture rises sometimes double. A well-fitting lid should be used, but it should not be sealed. Nearly all sources of information on sourdough emphasize that metal containers must not be used, except possibly for mixing. The acid in sourdough reacts on metal and could be toxic.

Amounts of flour given in these recipes are approximate and depend on the consistency of your starter. Maintain your starter at about the consistency of cake batter.

You can almost duplicate the bread flour used by bakeries by combining cake flour with all-purpose flour in the proportion of 1 part cake flour to 6 parts all-purpose flour.

## White Sandwich Loaf

1 1/2 cups starter
2 cups warm water
1/4 cup shortening, melted and cooled
About 6 cups flour
2 tablespoons sugar
2 teaspoons salt
1/2 teaspoon soda

In large mixing bowl, combine starter with warm water, mixing well. Stir in melted, cooled shortening. Sift 3 cups of the flour with sugar, salt and soda. Beat into liquid mixture. Blend in about 2 cups more flour, or enough to make a soft, workable dough. Turn out on board or cloth floured with remaining cup flour and knead for about 8 to 10 minutes, until smooth and satiny, working in additional flour as needed. Form dough into a ball.

Place dough in greased bowl, turn to grease both sides, cover and place in warm place, 80 to 85 degrees, and allow to rise until doubled, 2 hours or more. Punch down, form into 2 portions, kneading briefly each piece, and form into 2 loaves. Preferred method for shaping loaves is to roll or pat out into a rectangle, then roll up from 1 long side to the other, pinching tightly at each turn, then pinch edge well to to seal. Flatten ends and turn them under. Place loaves into 2 well-greased 9-by-5-inch loaf pans (or slightly smaller ones, if you have them). Brush tops with melted butter or oil and set to rise until not quite doubled, 2 hours or so. Bake at 400 degrees for about 45 minutes, or until done and brown. 2 loaves.

*Continued*

## Basic Dinner-Roll Sourdough

1 cup starter
1/2 cup milk, scalded
1/2 stick (1/4 cup) butter
1 tablespoon sugar
1 teaspoon salt
1/4 teaspoon soda
1 egg
3 cups flour, approximately

Place starter in large mixing bowl.

Scald milk, remove from heat and stir in butter, sugar and salt. Cool. Sift or stir soda with 2 cups of the flour. Add milk mixture to the starter. Beat in egg. Add the 2 cups flour with soda. Beat well. Turn out on board or cloth floured with remaining cup of flour. Knead several minutes, taking up flour as needed to form a soft dough. Form dough into ball, drop in greased bowl and turn to grease both sides. Cover and set to rise in warm place, 80 to 85 degrees, until doubled, about 2 hours. Punch down. After initial rising, form dough into 32 balls, dip tops in melted butter and place in 2 greased, 8-inch cake pans. Let rise in warm place until nearly double in size, then bake at 375 degrees for 15 minutes, or until done and brown.

Sweet rolls and kuchen may be made from this same basic dough, by increasing the amount of sugar to ¼ cup, and topping as desired.

## Sourdough Biscuits

1 cup starter
3/4 cup lukewarm milk
2 cups flour (approximately)
1/4 cup shortening
3/4 teaspoon salt
2 tablespoons baking powder
1/4 teaspoon soda

Stir the starter with milk in a mixing bowl. Sift or stir the flour with salt, baking powder and soda. Cut shortening into flour mixture with a pastry blender until particles are the size of tiny peas. Combine the two mixtures and stir well. Turn out on floured board or cloth and knead lightly. Work in a little more flour, if necessary, to make a soft workable dough. Roll out and cut with biscuit cutter. Set to rise for about an hour in warm place, 80 to 85 degrees. Bake at 400 degrees for 15 minutes or longer, until done and browned. About 2 dozen.

## Sourdough Waffles

1 cup starter
2 cups warm water (or milk)
3 cups flour, approximately
3 eggs
1/2 cup cooking oil
2 tablespoons sugar
1 teaspoon salt
1/4 teaspoon soda mixed with 1 tablespoon water

First, "set the sponge." The night before you bake the waffles, place the starter in large mixing bowl and beat in the water (or milk) and flour, alternately, beating until smooth. The batter should be considerably thicker than waffle batter at this point. Cover loosely and let stand at room temperature overnight. About an hour before serving, finish mixing: Beat in the eggs, oil, sugar, salt and soda. Let stand at least 30 minutes, preferably longer, before baking. Bake on hot waffle iron. Makes about 6 waffles. Leftover batter will still be good next morning, just cover and refrigerate.

## Dark Sandwich Bread

1 1/2 cups oatmeal, regular or quick-cooking
1/4 cup shortening
2 teaspoons salt
1/4 cup molasses (more if you like it on the sweet side)
2 cups boiling water
1 1/2 cups starter
1 1/2 cups graham flour
1/4 teaspoon soda
About 3 cups plain flour

In a large bowl, place oatmeal, shortening, salt and molasses. Pour the boiling water over and stir until shortening is dissolved. Cool to lukewarm and beat in the starter.

To complete the dough, stir the soda into the graham flour and beat into the first mixture. Then work in plain flour enough to give a good consistency for kneading. Turn out on floured board or cloth and knead until smooth and satiny for about 10 minutes. Place dough in greased bowl and turn so that surface is greased. Place bowl in plastic bag and set in warm place until doubled in bulk. Temperature should be about 85 degrees. Takes up to about 3 hours. Punch down, knead briefly and form 2 loaves. Place in 2 greased 9-by-5-by-4½-inch deep loaf pans. Brush tops with melted shortening or oil and let rise until almost doubled (about 2½ hours). Bake at 400 degrees 15 minutes, reduce heat to 350 and bake 35 to 40 minutes longer. 2 loaves.

# A Laudable Lasagna

What's better than lasagna, that grand champion casserole? Another lasagna, that's what! In this one, the noodles, instead of being stacked between layers of sauce, are rolled up with the cheese-egg mixture inside, then covered with meat sauce and baked.

### Lasagna Rolls

Bring 2 gallons of water to boiling, add 2 tablespoons salt and 2 tablespoons oil. Add 1 pound of wide lasanga noodles and cook 15 to 20 minutes. Drain and add cold water, allowing them to stand 5 minutes to cool. Drain again and make 2 neat stacks of them on a cookie sheet or cutting board. Cover with waxed paper till needed.

**The Meat Sauce:**
2 tablespoons oil
1 pound ground beef
1 large onion, chopped
2 cloves garlic, minced
1 teaspoon salt
1 teaspoon pepper
A 1-pound, 3-ounce can tomato purée
A 6-ounce can tomato paste
1/2 teaspoon oregano
2 cups water
1 teaspoon sugar, if desired
2 tablespoons chopped parsley

Heat oil in heavy saucepan. Add meat, onion and garlic. Sauté until brown. Add remaining ingredients and simmer 30 to 40 minutes. While sauce is simmering, make the cheese filling.

**The Cheese Filling:**
A 6-ounce package mozzarella cheese, grated
3 (12-ounce) cartons ricotta cheese (substitute sieved cottage cheese if necessary)
1/2 cup fine bread crumbs
1 teaspoon salt
1/2 teaspoon pepper
3 eggs, slightly beaten
1/3 cup chopped parsley

Combine all ingredients and mix well with a fork. To assemble:

Cut down through the 2 stacks of noodles, halving them crosswise. Fill each half-noodle with cheese filling and roll up, placing them in an oiled 3-quart casserole, alternating layers of rolls with meat sauce. (Add a little water to sauce if it seems necessary toward the last.) When casserole is completed, sprinkle with Parmesan or Romano cheese, cover with foil, and bake at 375 degrees 30 to 40 minutes. May be made up a day ahead. Or freeze it, well-wrapped. Serves 10 to 12.

# The Moister Oyster

As a main dish, fried oysters are easy to do and mighty hard to beat. Try serving them heaped in an edible bowl: a loaf of bread that has been slightly hollowed, coated inside with butter and herbs, then toasted.

## Shrimp Bisque

3 tablespoons butter or margarine
1 medium onion, sliced
2 celery stalks, sliced
1/2 carrot, sliced
1 tomato, quartered
3 cups water
1 bay leaf
Salt, pepper to taste
1 slice lemon
2 pounds shrimp
1/2 cup sherry (or use an extra 1/2 cup water)
1 cup heavy cream

Melt butter in saucepan, add vegetables and cook until tender. Add water, bay leaf, seasonings, and lemon slice. Bring to a boil. Add shrimp and ¼ cup of the wine. Simmer 30 minutes. Let shrimp cool in stock. Discard bay leaf, and lemon. Then, using a blender or food mill, purée the mixture. Remove to the top of a double boiler. Add remaining wine and cream. Bring to serving temperature over hot water. Serves 8.

## Oyster Crown Loaf

*To prepare the loaf:*

Remove a slice from the top of a loaf of unsliced white bread. Remove enough bread from inside the top of the loaf to make a bed about an inch deep for the finished oysters. Soften half a stick of margarine or butter, ¼ cup, and butter the hollowed place. Sprinkle ½ teaspoon of thyme and ½ teaspoon of oregano over the butter. Ten minutes before serving, put the loaf into a 450-degree oven to get very hot and a little brown on top.

*To fry the oysters:*

(1½ pints or two 12-ounce cans of select oysters will serve 8. Or use standard-size oysters; just roll 3 or 4 at a time to make big ones.)

3/4 pound soda crackers, rolled fine or ground
3 eggs, beaten with 3 tablespoons water
2 teaspoons salt

Gently stir the salt through the oysters with the hands. An opened newspaper makes a good working surface. Make an assembly line of the oysters, the beaten eggs, the cracker crumbs and a flat dish or pan for the breaded oysters. Pick up one or more oysters at a time (they will merge into one after breading, so make them the size you want) and roll them first in cracker meal, then in egg, then in the crumbs again. Press to make the coating really stick so they won't lose their coats while frying.

The breading may be done several hours in advance of the frying and the oysters kept in the refrigerator till needed. To fry, heat ½ inch of vegetable shortening in a skillet. Put in oysters without crowding them and fry, turning only once, to brown on both sides. They will cook thoroughly in only 10 or 12 minutes. Overcooking dries out the juices. Drain on absorbent paper. Heap into the prepared hot loaf of bread. Serve hot, with tartar or cocktail sauce.

*Tartar Sauce:*

Combine ¾ cup mayonnaise with 1 tablespoon chopped capers, 1 or 2 teaspoons minced onion, 1 tablespoon lemon juice and a dash of Worcestershire sauce.

*Cocktail Sauce:*

Combine ¾ cup catsup or chili sauce with 1 to 2 tablespoons horseradish, a few drops Tabasco and 1 tablespoon lemon juice.

## Lime Chiffon Pie

1 envelope gelatin
1/4 cup water
3 egg yolks
1/2 cup sugar
1/8 teaspoon salt
1/2 cup lime juice
1 teaspoon grated lime rind
3 egg whites
1/2 cup sugar
Whipped cream for garnish, with a little sugar added

Prepare baked pie shell. Soften gelatin in water. Place 3 egg yolks, ½ cup sugar and salt in double boiler, and cook over hot water, stirring constantly until thickened. Add gelatin to hot custard and stir to dissolve. Stir in lime juice and grated rind. Cool. Beat egg whites until stiff and gradually add ½ cup sugar, blending thoroughly. Fold egg whites into cooled custard. Turn into pie shell, chill and garnish with sweetened whipped cream.

# A Tenderloin Dilly

When you bake the succulent tenderloin of pork in a blend of consommé, tomato and cream, you've got a masterpiece. Add a whiff of dill and it becomes irresistible.

### Pork Tenderloin Baked in Dill Cream

1- to 1 1/2-pound piece pork tenderloin
2 tablespoons butter
2 tablespoons oil
1 clove garlic, split
1/2 pound fresh mushrooms, lightly sautéed in butter
  (or substitute canned ones)
1 can consommé
1 cup tomatoes, fresh and peeled or canned ones,
  drained, or a basket of cocktail tomatoes
Salt and pepper to taste
A few sprigs fresh parsley, chopped, or 1 teaspoon dried
2 teaspoons dill seed
1/2 cup heavy cream

Heat the butter and oil in a skillet and add the garlic. Shake skillet to permit garlic flavor to permeate the fat, then remove garlic when it is brown. Add the pork tenderloin and brown it well on all sides. Transfer meat to casserole or heavy oven-going pan with tight-fitting lid, then add mushrooms, consommé, tomatoes, salt, pepper, parsley and dill seed.

Cover and bake at 350 degrees for 1½ hours. Add cream and continue baking, uncovered, for another ½ hour, or until meat is very tender, basting 2 or 3 times as it browns.

Remove meat to a warm platter and thicken the pan sauce, if needed, with a little flour mixed with cold water. Serve the meat, sliced, right in the sauce, or put the sauce in a gravy boat for passing. Serves 6.

### Stuffed Turnips à la Pearl

8 medium turnips
2 tablespoons butter or margarine
1 teaspoon salt
2 teaspoons sugar
1 tablespoon minced onion
1/8 teaspoon pepper
Paprika

Peel and boil turnips in salt water until tender. Do not overcook. Drain well. Immediately cut slice from top of each. Then with tip of spoon, carefully remove center without breaking shells.

Mash well, adding seasoning. Pile back into shells and dust with paprika. Place in buttered pan and bake about 25 minutes at 350 degrees or until lightly browned.

### Smashed Radishes

About 2 dozen radishes
1/4 teaspoon salt
1 tablespoon soy sauce
2 tablespoons vinegar
1 teaspoon sugar
1/2 teaspoon salt
1 teaspoon salad oil

Wash and trim radishes. Lay each on its side, then crush by pounding it decisively once or twice with a heavy cleaver or bottom of a glass. They should split open but not break in two. Sprinkle with salt (¼ teaspoon) and let stand 10 minutes. Drain. Combine soy sauce, vinegar, sugar and remaining salt. Add to radishes and toss gently. Chill. Sprinkle with the oil just before serving. Use on relish dish with sliced cucumbers, green pepper, green onions. Or place a few on a lettuce leaf for a small individual salad. 6 servings.

### Louisiana Yam Pie

1 9-inch pie shell, baked
1 tablespoon (1 envelope) unflavored gelatin
1/2 cup juice from yams
1 (1 pound) can yams in orange-pineapple sauce
3 egg yolks
1/4 cup milk
3/4 cup brown sugar
1/2 teaspoon salt
1 teaspoon cinnamon
1/4 teaspoon ginger
1/4 teaspoon allspice
3 egg whites
1/4 teaspoon cream of tartar
6 tablespoons granulated sugar
1 cup heavy cream, whipped and sweetened

Soften gelatin in the ½-cup yam juice. Mash yams thoroughly and combine with egg yolks, milk, brown sugar, salt and spices in a saucepan. Bring to boil over low heat. Boil 1 minute, stirring constantly. Remove from heat and stir in softened gelatin. Chill until partially set, then beat until smooth.

Combine egg whites and cream of tartar, beat until stiff. Gradually add sugar to egg whites. Fold meringue gently into yam mixture. Place in pie shell and chill for at least 2 hours or overnight. Garnish with sweetened whipped cream.

# The Fairest Fowl

Here's a trio of recipes to prove, as if anyone needed proof, that there's no reason ever to tire of chicken. Each dish is better than the other, except for the North Woods Chicken and Beans, which is simply out of this world!

## Spanish Roast Chicken

A 5-pound roasting chicken with giblets
4 cups boiling salted water
1 cup melted butter or margarine
1/2 cup chopped onions
1/2 pound chopped mushrooms
4 cups soft bread crumbs
1 cup pimiento-stuffed olives, sliced
1/2 teaspoon poultry seasoning
1/4 teaspoon thyme
1 teaspoon salt
Boiling water
3 tablespoons cornstarch
1/8 teaspoon pepper

Cook giblets, covered, in boiling salted water 35 to 45 minutes, or until tender. Drain and reserve stock; chop giblets. Heat ½ cup melted butter and add mushrooms and onions; cook over low heat until tender. Add bread crumbs, ½ cup sliced olives, poultry seasoning, thyme and ½ teaspoon salt. Cook until crumbs are lightly browned. Add boiling water to reserved stock to make 3¾ cups. Add ¾ cup stock to crumb mixture. Cool. Rub chicken cavity with ½ teaspoon salt. Fill cavity loosely with olive stuffing. Fasten opening with skewers. Place on rack in shallow roasting pan; brush with some of the remaining ½ cup melted butter. Bake in a 325-degree oven about 2½ hours, or until meat thermometer registers 190 degrees. Baste with remaining melted butter frequently.

Slowly add ½ cup stock to cornstarch and pepper; stir until smooth. Stir in broth for the gravy. Add giblets and remaining ½ cup olives.

## Chicken Creole

1 3 1/2-pound frying chicken
1 No. 2 can tomatoes
2 tablespoons butter
1 teaspoon salt
Few grains pepper
Few grains cayenne pepper
1 sprig thyme
1 tablespoon minced parsley
1 bay leaf
3 cloves garlic, minced
1 tablespoon flour
6 chopped shallots, or 1/2 cup minced onion
5 tablespoons chopped green pepper
1/2 cup white wine

Cook chicken in water until done. Cut into bite-sized pieces. Combine tomatoes and 1 tablespoon butter, simmer 10 minutes, stirring occasionally. Add salt, pepper and cayenne, cook 10 minutes. Add parsley, thyme, bay leaf and garlic. Cook 15 minutes, or until sauce is thick. In separate skillet melt 1 tablespoon butter, blend in flour, and cook, stirring until brown. Add shallots, green pepper, brown lightly. Add wine, stirring constantly, until slightly thickened. Add to tomato sauce, then add chicken and cover. Simmer 45 minutes, or until chicken is tender. If desired, place chicken on rice, garnish with avocado slices and parsley. Serves 4 to 6.

## North Woods Chicken and Beans

2 pounds dry navy beans
A 5-pound fat hen cut in serving pieces or equivalent weight of chicken pieces
2 medium onions with 2 or 3 cloves stuck in them
1/4 pound salt pork cut in 1/2-inch cubes (more if chicken is not fat)
Salt and pepper to taste
1/2 teaspoon dry mustard
1/2 teaspoon garlic salt (optional)
Hot water

Soak beans overnight. Drain and place a third of the beans in bottom of a large 4-quart casserole. Sprinkle with salt and pepper, place onions and the salt pork on bean layer. Add another third of the beans, salt and pepper again, then lay the chicken pieces on. Add remaining beans and more salt and pepper, mustard and garlic salt, if used. Add hot water to cover. Cover closely, place in oven at 200 degrees and bake 18 hours.

The only attention the casserole requires during this long, slow cooking is the addition of water occasionally. Two hours before serving, pull up the chicken pieces and remove the bones, then gently stir chicken back into the beans so that each serving will contain an honest share of everything. One hour before serving, remove the cover; the finished product should be nice and moist without being soupy.

# Sassy Sauerbraten

Made at a leisurely pace and served with dumplings, sauerbraten confronts one at table with an aroma so robust and tempting as to awaken the most jaded appetite. The sauerbraten recipe may be used with venison, rabbit or tongue, as well as with beef roast.

### Sauerbraten

5-pound beef rump or roast

*Vegetable Marinade:*

2 pounds carrots
1 onion
1 bay leaf
2 pounds celery
4 or 5 peppercorns
2 slices lemon
Salt to taste
1 quart water
1 cup vinegar

*Gravy:*

3 tablespoons shortening
3 tablespoons flour
2 tablespoons sugar
1/4 to 1/3 cup sugar, caramelized
1 tablespoon lemon juice
1 teaspoon prepared mustard
1/2 cup sour cream

Slice the vegetables for the marinade ¼-inch thick and put them into a pot with all the other ingredients except the vinegar. Cook until vegetables are tender. Cool and mix in the vinegar.

Place the meat in plastic or pottery container, pour the vegetable marinade over it, adding water if there is not enough liquid to cover. Refrigerate, covered, 5 to 7 days, turning the meat daily.

Take out the meat. Drain and reserve liquid from the vegetables. Melt 3 tablespoons shortening in large kettle, add the meat and drained vegetables. Add enough of the reserved liquid, adding more from time to time, to make plenty of steam, and cook the meat, covered, until tender. Remove meat.

To finish, prepare gravy by cooking the vegetables down until all the liquid is gone and only the shortening remains. Sprinkle with flour and sugar and cook, stirring constantly, until mixture is well browned. Pour the remaining liquid from the marinade into browned mixture and boil for 3 to 4 minutes. Then run through a sieve or put through the blender, until smooth. Return to pan.

Caramelize ¼ to 1/3 cup sugar by melting in a small iron skillet and add to gravy. Add lemon juice and mustard. Taste and add salt if needed. Add sour cream. Slice the meat, put it into the sauce and heat all together, very hot without actually boiling. Serve with dumplings. Or macaroni is good with the sauerbraten.

### Sauerbraten Dumplings

2 cups flour
2 tablespoons shortening
3 eggs, beaten
1/2 teaspoon salt
1/2 cup water or more, to make a not-very-stiff dough
4 or 5 slices bread cut into 1/2-inch cubes and browned in butter

Mix flour with salt and cut in the shortening. Add beaten eggs and enough water to form dough. Stir in bread cubes. Bring 4 quarts water to boil in a large kettle. Add 1 tablespoon salt. Form dough into small round balls or simply drop by teaspoonfuls into rapidly boiling water, taking care not to crowd them. Cook 10 to 15 minutes or until done. (Best test is to cut one open and see if it's done.) Drain well and place on a warmed serving dish, dot with butter and keep warm until all are cooked and ready to serve.

### Kartoffel Klosse

4 large potatoes
1 teaspoon flour
1 teaspoon salt
1 teaspoon parsley
2 slices bread, cut in 1/2-inch cubes and browned in butter

Boil potatoes until tender. Mash or grind them with the flour, salt and parsley. Form potato mixture into balls, secreting a toasted bread cube in the center of each one. Bring 4 quarts water to boil in large kettle, add 1 tablespoon salt. Drop balls into boiling water. They will float when done. Serve Kartoffel Klosse with sauerbraten and gravy.

# For Chili Days

Rx for the blah feeling you get on a wintry day: take steaming hot chili until relief is obtained. Think of fellow sufferers and invite them in too, and make a meal of it with grilled ham-and-Swiss sandwiches and other good things.

## Chili

1/2 pound pinto beans
5 cups canned tomatoes
1 pound chopped green pepper (2 1/2 cups)
1 1/2 tablespoons salad oil
1 1/2 pounds chopped onions (4 cups)
2 cloves garlic, crushed
1/2 cup chopped parsley
1/2 cup butter or margarine
1 1/2 pounds ground chuck
1 pound ground pork
1/3 cup chili powder
2 tablespoons salt
1 1/2 teaspoons pepper
1 1/2 teaspoons cumin seed
1 1/2 teaspoons monosodium glutamate

Soak beans overnight. Simmer tender for 1 hour, add tomatoes, and cook 5 minutes. Sauté green pepper and onion in the oil until tender. Add garlic and parsley.

Melt butter in a large heavy-bottomed kettle and sauté the meat in it for 15 minutes. Add onion mixture. Add chili powder and cook 10 minutes. Add beans and spices. Simmer 1 hour or more. Skim fat from top. Serve very hot. Recipe makes 1 gallon.

## Grilled Swiss 'n' Ham

2 4 1/2-ounce cans deviled ham
1 teaspoon very hot mustard
8 slices Swiss cheese
16 slices white bread
Soft butter to spread on for grilling

Mix ham with mustard. Spread all bread slices with a thin coating of the deviled ham. Arrange the Swiss cheese on eight of the bread slices and cover with the other eight. Spread outside layers of bread thinly with soft butter, place on grill, buttered sides down. Spread top sides with butter, then proceed to grill until the cheese melts and the bread is nicely browned. Cut the sandwiches immediately into quarters and stand the pieces up, so they won't get soggy. Makes 8 sandwiches.

## Tarragon Green Salad

8 cups mixed greens, torn into bite-sized pieces, washed and well drained
2 large tomatoes, cut in wedges, drained
1 cup sliced black olives
1 cup sour cream (or sour half-and-half)
5 teaspoons tarragon vinegar
1 teaspoon sugar
1/2 teaspoon salt
2 teaspoons minced onions

Combine greens, tomatoes and black olives in large salad bowl. Mix together the remainder of the ingredients and toss with the greens at serving time. Serves 8.

## Apple Crunch Dessert

1 can (1 pound, 4 ounces) pie-sliced apples, or 4 cups sliced, peeled apples
1/2 cup sugar
2 tablespoons orange-flavored instant breakfast drink
1 tablespoon quick-cooking tapioca
1 tablespoon butter, melted
1/4 teaspoon salt
1/4 teaspoon ground cinnamon

Blend all ingredients together in 1½-quart baking dish. Place aside.

*Topping:*

1/4 cup butter
1/2 cup sugar
1/4 cup orange-flavored instant breakfast drink
2 tablespoons flour
1 1/2 cups crisp whole-wheat flakes, or use 2 cups corn flakes and increase sugar to 2/3 cup (crush corn flakes slightly before adding to butter mixture)

Soften butter. Blend in sugar, instant breakfast drink and the flour. Stir in cereal and spread over apple mixture in baking dish. Cover and bake at 375 degrees for 15 minutes. Remove cover and bake 15 minutes longer. Serve warm with cream. Makes five or six servings.

# A Glow to the Chops

Vermouth in the skillet with pork chops? Absolutely. By the time these marvelous chops reach the table, all the alcohol has evaporated, leaving only a mysterious essence. A noble dish!

### Pork Chops Martini

8 double-thick pork chops
Salt and pepper to taste
1 tablespoon shortening
1 cup dry vermouth
1 1/2 teaspoons dill weed
1 teaspoon cornstarch mixed with 1/4 cup water

Rub salt and pepper into both sides of the chops and brown in the shortening in a heavy skillet. Reduce heat, add the vermouth and dill weed and simmer 1 hour. Remove the chops, add the cornstarch water and boil up for 2 or 3 minutes. Glaze the chops and serve.

### Dorzbach Potato Poufs

2 cups mashed potatoes, seasoned with salt (leftovers may be used)
Salt to taste
2 eggs
2 tablespoons pancake mix
2 tablespoons flour, more or less
1/2 teaspoon nutmeg
Oil or shortening for deep frying

Beat the eggs into the mashed potatoes. Add the pancake mix, salt and nutmeg, mixing well. Add enough of the flour to make a consistency that will allow you to pick up the "dough" on a teaspoon and drop it into the hot fat. (Use a second teaspoon to push the potato off.) Fry only a few at a time and watch them; they brown quickly. Turn them once during the frying. Drain on paper towels and serve hot with chops. (Children like them coated with powdered sugar, like doughnuts.)

### Stuffed Zucchini

8 small whole zucchini
1 small onion, chopped
3 tablespoons butter or margarine
1/2 cup chopped celery
1/2 cup green pepper
1 cup drained canned tomatoes
1 teaspoon salt
1 teaspoon oregano

Plunge the whole zucchini into a kettle of boiling, salted water. Turn off the heat and let cool in the liquid a few minutes. Melt butter in skillet and stir-fry the chopped vegetables until barely tender. Season with the teaspoon salt and oregano. Scoop out some flesh from zucchini, leaving a good solid shell. Chop some of the scoopings into the vegetable mixture and pile the filling into the zucchini. Put in shallow greased casserole and bake 45 minutes at 350 degrees. Serves 8.

### Shrimp Dressing for Green Salad

1 cup sour cream
1/4 teaspoon salt
1/4 cup chili sauce
2 tablespoons drained pickle relish
1 tablespoon minced onion
5 ounces cooked shrimp, diced
1 teaspoon lemon juice

Combine ingredients and chill thoroughly. If it seems heavy, thin with 3 or 4 tablespoons light cream. Makes about 2 cups dressing. Serve over wedges of head lettuce. This recipe is very low in calories, about 31 per tablespoon.

### Riz pour Entrements (Dessert Rice)

2 cups milk
1-inch length of vanilla bean, or 1 teaspoon vanilla extract
2 cups minute rice
1/4 teaspoon salt
4 tablespoons butter
6 egg yolks, beaten

Boil the milk with the vanilla bean, just an instant, then remove from heat. Add rice and stir in gently. Cover and let stand 15 minutes. Put pan on low heat and stir in the beaten egg yolks, being careful not to destroy the shape of the rice grains. (If you are using vanilla extract, add it now.) Put in oiled individual molds or shape with your hands. Here's a delicious topping:

*Poached Pears with Cherry Sauce*

4 fresh pears
1 can frozen cherries
1 cup sugar
Juice from cherries plus water to make 2 cups liquid
Red food color, just a few drops
2 tablespoons cornstarch mixed with 3 tablespoons water

Peel, halve and core the pears. Boil liquid with sugar and red color until it becomes a thin syrup. Carefully poach the pears until just tender. Remove the pears and chill. Add the cherries to the liquid, add cornstarch-water and cook 5 minutes, then chill.

In individual dessert dishes, place a mound of dessert rice, top each with a poached pear half and spoon cherry sauce over all. 8 servings.

# Via the Grapevine

Just because chicken is so available and so economical is no reason to sell it short. Here's a reminder that chicken can rise to exotic heights. Almonds and seedless green grapes (canned ones if necessary) are the magic wands.

### Chicken with Grapes

4 large chicken breasts, halved
2 pounds seedless green grapes
1 pound fresh mushrooms, or 2 large cans
1/2 cup blanched whole almonds
1/2 cup flour
1 teaspoon salt
1/2 teaspoon pepper
1 teaspoon paprika

Coat the chicken pieces in the flour which has been mixed with the salt, pepper and paprika. Place in a buttered baking pan, skin side up. Set oven at 250 degrees and bake chicken uncovered 1 hour, turning after the first ½ hour. After the hour has elapsed, turn chicken again and sprinkle all over with the grapes, mushrooms and almonds. Cover closely and continue baking 2 hours longer. Makes 8 servings.

### Cranberry-Cottage Cheese Mold

1 pound can whole cranberry sauce
1 pound cottage cheese
1 package lemon-flavored gelatin
1 cup boiling water
1 tablespoon lemon juice

Dissolve the gelatin in 1 cup boiling water; add lemon juice. Break up the cranberry sauce in a bowl. Sieve the cottage cheese or, preferably, puree it in a blender. Put half the cooled gelatin mixture in the cranberry sauce, and the other half in the sieved cottage cheese. Into an oiled 6-cup mold, spoon the two mixtures alternately to get a marbleized effect. It also can make 8 to 10 individual molds. Refrigerate till set. Unmold on lettuce.

### Lemon Cake with Apricot Glaze

1 box lemon cake mix, 2-layer size
1 box lemon instant pudding
4 eggs
1 cup water
3/4 cup salad oil

In large bowl of your mixer, beat the eggs, water and oil together. Add the cake and pudding mixes and beat 5 minutes at medium speed. Pour batter into 2 greased and floured 9-inch layer pans and bake 30 minutes at 350 degrees. Or bake in sheet-cake pan about 10 by 14 inches for 35 to 40 minutes, or until it tests done. You can put layers together and top the cake with a jar of apricot jam from the pantry shelf for a quick job. A good topping for the cake baked on a sheet is:

3 tablespoons salad oil
2 cups sifted powdered sugar, or more to make spreadable
Juice and rind of 1 lemon

Simply mix and spread on cake. For variations use chocolate-cake mix and chocolate pudding, or spice-cake mix with butterscotch pudding.

Topping for either variation may be made by combining oil and powdered sugar with 2 tablespoons cocoa or 2 teaspoons dry instant coffee, flavored with vanilla, and thinned to spreadability by adding a little milk or hot water.

R. BRIGGS

# Mardi Gras Morsels

Mardi Gras, "Fat Tuesday," is the final feast before the fasting of Lent begins on Ash Wednesday. This meal would probably taste even better if one could go to New Orleans to eat it!

## Chicken Gumbo

A 6-pound fat hen
Salt and pepper to taste
1/4 cup shortening
5 tablespoons flour
1 cup finely chopped onion
6 green onions, chopped, tops and all
3 cups sliced okra, fresh or frozen
1 cup chopped celery
1/2 green pepper, chopped
1/2 cup chopped fresh parsley
4 quarts boiling water
3 cups canned tomatoes
1/2 teaspoon thyme
2 cloves garlic, minced
1/2-pound slice of ham, diced
More salt and pepper to taste
Filé powder to taste

Melt shortening in bottom of large heavy kettle. Cut chicken into serving pieces; sprinkle with salt and pepper, then brown, turning to cook evenly, in shortening. Remove chicken. Add flour to fat in pan and stir until nicely browned. Add onions, both plain and green ones, okra, celery, garlic, green pepper and parsley. Cook, stirring, for 10 minutes. Place chicken back in pan with vegetables, add water, tomatoes, thyme and ham. Simmer about 2 hours, or until chicken is very tender. About ½ hour before it is done, take out chicken, remove bones and replace meat in gumbo. Adjust seasonings. Serve in soup bowls and let each person add filé powder to his own taste. Never cook the filé powder in the gumbo. A simple green salad goes nicely alongside.

## Creole Sweet Potato Rolls

A 1-pound, 10-ounce can sweet potatoes (2 cups), and their liquid
1 cup milk, scalded and cooled to lukewarm
1/4 cup warm water
1/2 envelope dry yeast or 1/2 cake yeast
1 tablespoon butter, melted
1 teaspoon salt
About 2 1/2 cups flour

Sieve sweet potatoes, along with enough of liquid to make 2 cups. Dissolve yeast in warm water and add, along with butter and salt, to milk. Stir well. Add sieved sweet potatoes and beat well. Add enough flour to form a soft dough. Knead on floured board or cloth 5 minutes, or until very smooth. Cover with a bowl and let rest 20 minutes.

Roll dough into rectangle about 15 by 18 inches. It will be 1/3- to 1/2-inch thick. Cut in rounds. Dip both sides in melted butter or shortening and place close together, folding rolls in half as you go, on 11-by-16-inch baking pan. Let rise about an hour (or until light) in a warm place. Bake at 400 degrees for about 15 minutes or until lightly browned and done through. Makes about 6 dozen small rolls.

## Molasses Pie

2 8-inch pie shells, partially baked (8 minutes at 425 degrees)
2 cups molasses or sorghum
Juice of 2 lemons
4 eggs, separated
1/2 cup sugar
2 tablespoons flour mixed with water to a paste
1/2 teaspoon cinnamon
1/4 teaspoon nutmeg
2 tablespoons butter, melted

Blend molasses with lemon juice. Add flour and water paste and mix thoroughly. Beat in spices and butter. Beat egg yolks with sugar until light and lemon-colored. Blend into molasses mixture. Beat egg whites and fold in last. Pour into 2 pie shells and bake 30 minutes at 350 degrees, or until set.

Note: The New Orleans-style molasses called for in the old original recipe might be a little strong for most tastes. While some like it very much, others prefer a lighter-flavored sorghum.

R. BRIGGS

# Christmas Cookies

Exquisite Scandinavian cookies, baked by the hundreds and stored in tins, are perfect to have at Christmas, either to lavish on the family or to wrap up as gifts. You can also bake a towering Danish Kransekage, even without the traditional pans from Denmark, with these instructions.

## Kransekage

3 pounds almond paste
4 egg whites
4 cups confectioners' sugar
6 tablespoons lemon juice (a little more or less)

In a large, heavy saucepan, thoroughly blend the almond paste with the unbeaten egg whites. Put pan over low heat and mix with a wooden spoon until warm and smooth. Turn mixture into a bowl. On pastry board sprinkled with confectioners' sugar, using the palms of your hands, shape the almond paste into 12 pencil-shaped rolls, ½-inch thick. Cut the rolls into lengths: 5, 6, 7, 8, 10, 12, 14, 16, 18, 20, 22 and 24 inches. On greased baking sheets, form each length of paste into a ring, sealing ends together. Pinch the tops of the rings into a ridge on top. Measure and reshape a bit if necessary, so that you have rings these sizes in diameter: 2, 2½, 3, 3½, 4, 4½, 5, 5½, 6, 6½, 7, and 7½ inches.

Bake the rings 20 to 25 minutes, or until light golden. Remove from oven and cool on the baking sheets. Make icing by blending the lemon juice into the confectioners' sugar. Decorate each ring with zigzag lines as pictured. The rings may be stored in tin boxes after they are dry, and kept until needed.

To assemble: Use a large serving plate or cake stand and, starting with the largest ring, build up the pyramid.

## Finsk Brod

*(Finnish Shortbread)*

1/4 lb. butter
1/4 lb. margarine
3 cups flour
1/3 cup sugar, plus 1 tablespoon

Garnish:

1 egg white
25 almonds, chopped
4 tablespoons sugar

Work butter, margarine and flour together. Then add sugar. Roll out in long, slender rolls from ½ to 1 inch in diameter. Cut these rolls into 1½- to 2-inch lengths. Dip each length into egg white, which has been whipped with an equal amount of water. Then dip in mixed sugar and almonds. Place on greased cookie sheets.

Bake 10 to 15 minutes in 350-degree oven, or until as brown as you prefer. Remove to racks to cool.

## Pebbernodder (Peppernuts)

6 tablespoons light corn syrup
1/2 cup light-brown sugar
1/2 lb. margarine
1/2 teaspoon baking soda
1/2 teaspoon cream of tartar
1 lb. flour
1 teaspoon cinnamon
1 teaspoon cloves

Warm syrup. Add margarine. Cool slightly, then add other ingredients. Mix well. Roll into long strips about a half inch in diameter. Cut into small pieces—about ¼-inch lengths—and drop on buttered baking sheet. Bake about 12 minutes in 325-degree oven. Must be kept in tightly closed tins, after they are cool. Yield: 350 cookies.

## Pecan Crescents

1/4 lb. butter
1/4 lb. margarine
2 cups flour
4 tablespoons confectioners' sugar
3/4 cup pecan pieces

Work together first four ingredients. Add nuts. Shape into crescents, using about 1 teaspoon of dough. Bake about 20 minutes in 350-degree oven. Yield: 56 cookies.

## Sylkakor

*(Butter Leaves with Jelly)*

1 cup butter
1/2 cup sugar
1 egg yolk
1 teaspoon bitter-almond extract
2 1/2 cups flour

Garnish:

1 egg white
25 almonds, chopped fine
4 tablespoons sugar

Also:

Jelly or preserves

Work butter and sugar until creamy and fluffy. Add egg yolk, bitter almond and flour, and mix thoroughly. Roll out thin on floured pastry cloth and cut in round cakes. Cut hole in half of cakes, brush with egg white and sprinkle with mixed almond and sugar. Place all cookies on buttered

*Continued*

baking sheet and bake in 350-degree oven from 8 to 10 minutes or until golden yellow. Cool. Spread the solid cookies with jam and place a "holey" cookie on top of each. Yield: 34 cookies.

### Kleiner

3 eggs
1 cup sugar
1/2 teaspoon salt
4 tablespoons cream
1/2 cup butter
1 teaspoon baking powder
4 cups flour
1 teaspoon (heaping) cardamon
3 to 4 quarts cooking oil

Beat eggs and sugar, add cream, and melted butter. Then stir in flour, salt, baking powder and cardamon. (Exact amount of flour may vary, according to size of eggs. Dough should be soft, but not sticky—and stiff enough to roll out like cookies.) Roll out to ¼-inch thickness on pastry cloth or lightly floured board. Cut into diamonds about three inches long with a slit in the center. Pass one end of the diamond through this slit. Drop the kleiner into hot deep fat. When the underside is brown, flip the kleiner over in the fat. It is best to cook only 6 to 8 at a time, turning with a kitchen fork or a metal knitting needle. When both sides are light brown, remove the kleiner from the fat and let cool on a clean piece of brown wrapping paper. Yield: 100 cookies.

### Vanilla Kranse

1/2 lb. butter
1/4 lb. margarine
1/2 lb. (1 cup) sugar
1 egg
1 teaspoon vanilla
1 lb. flour

Soften butter and margarine to room temperature. Add sugar and blend well. Mix in egg and vanilla. Then add flour and mix well. Using cookie press, press onto ungreased cookie sheets. Bake 10 to 15 minutes (or as you prefer) in 350-degree oven. Remove from pans while still warm. Yield: 123 cookies.

### Brune Kager (Brown Cookies)

1 cup granulated sugar
1 cup molasses
1/3 cup butter or margarine
1 egg
1 teaspoon soda
1 teaspoon baking powder
4 cups flour

Cream butter and sugar. Add egg, molasses and sifted dry ingredients. Knead together. Let rest in a cool place at least an hour. Roll thin and cut into different shapes such as round, diamond or strips. Bake 10 to 15 minutes in 350-degree oven. Yield: 150 cookies.

### Decorated Christmas Cookies

1 cup shortening
2/3 cup sugar
3/4 teaspoon salt
2 teaspoons vanilla
Exactly 1/3 cup eggs (1 to 2, depending on size). A little water may be added for required measurement.
3 cups sifted all-purpose flour

Combine shortening, sugar, salt, flavoring and eggs. Beat until smooth and light. Stir in flour. Pat dough to about 1-inch thickness and wrap in waxed paper. Chill dough at least 2 hours. Don't move dough from refrigerator until everything else is ready.

Preheat oven to 350 degrees. Use pastry cloth and covered rolling pin. Roll dough to ¼- to 3/8-inch thickness (using only about ¼ of dough at a time). Flour inside of contour cookie cutters. Cut cookie. Press shape into cookies. Unmold on ungreased cookie sheets. Bake 12 to 15 minutes. Do not allow to brown. Remove to cool on racks before decorating. Yield: About 26 cookies.

# Christmas Candy

All it takes to make good candy at home is a couple of basic tools and the raw materials. The first essential is a good candy thermometer. A marble slab, while not necessary for all candies, makes the difference when there's fondant to be worked or brittle to be poured for quick cooling.

### Good Basic Caramel

2 cups sugar
1 cup light corn syrup
2 cups heavy cream, warm
1/2 teaspoon salt
1/2 teaspoon vanilla

In a heavy-bottomed 3-quart saucepan, mix together sugar, syrup and 1 cup of the cream.

Cook about 10 minutes, stirring thoroughly to dissolve the sugar before it comes to a strong boil. Insert thermometer. Thereafter, stir only if it seems necessary to prevent scorching. Add the other cup of cream very slowly, so as not to stop the cooking. When the thermometer reaches 230 degrees, cook more slowly to 244 degrees.

Remove pan from heat and add the salt and vanilla, stirring just enough to blend flavors.

For nut caramels, add a cup of broken nuts, turn candy into an oiled pan 8-inches square; place on cooling rack. When cold, turn out on cutting board and cut into squares. Wrap each piece in waxed paper.

## Modjeskas

    1 batch of Basic Caramel
    36-40 marshmallows

Pour the caramel, as soon as it has been flavored and stirred, onto oiled marble. Cut the marshmallows in half with wet scissors. When the caramel has cooled, use candy scraper or spatula to pick up a small sheet of caramel and wrap each marshmallow-half, molding with oiled fingers to cover. Or let caramel cool 10 minutes in pan, then dip marshmallows, using a sharp fork. As marshmllows are covered, line them up on oiled marble to finish cooling. Wrap each separately in waxed paper cut 4-by-5-inches. Store in tight tin boxes. Makes 72-80 Modjeskas, depending on how thickly the caramel is applied.

## Pecan Rolls
## with Opera-Cream Centers

    1 batch of Basic Caramel
    2 lbs. broken pecan meats
Opera Cream Ingredients:
    4 cups sugar
    2 tablespoons light corn syrup
    2 cups hot coffee cream
    1/4 teaspoon salt
    1 teaspoon vanilla

Using a 4-quart, heavy-bottomed saucepan cook the sugar, syrup and 1 cup of the cream for about 10 minutes, stirring with a wooden spoon only until the sugar is dissolved. (Leave the spoon in the candy. Use only to prevent boiling over or scorching, stirring only across the bottom of the pan.) Insert thermometer. Over high heat, add the other cup of cream very slowly so the boiling won't stop. Lower heat and cook gently to 240 degrees.

Pour the candy on lightly oiled marble slab. Cool to about 125 degrees. Sprinkle on the salt and vanilla. Cream it with scraper until of soft-fudge consistency. As soon as it holds its shape, knead, scraping the candy with the scraper held in one hand, working the candy with the other, until it is creamy. (If the candy should become too hard to knead, scrape it into a lump and cover it with waxed paper, a damp towel and a bowl. Knead after 15 minutes.) Pack candy in an 8-inch-square pan. Opera cream is best if refrigerated

several days before using.

When ready to assemble pecan rolls, take opera cream from refrigerator and cut it into 8 long pieces. Gently roll each piece between the hands to make a long round center. Make a flat pile of about a fourth of the chopped pecans on marble slab or other working surface. Have your pan of still-warm cooked caramel alongside. Lay an opera-cream center on the nuts and spoon caramel on top. Turn the roll so the caramel is coated with nuts. Spoon on caramel and turn 2 or 3 more times until entire roll is thickly covered with caramel and nuts. Wrap tightly in waxed paper and refrigerate. Slice to serve. Makes 8 rolls, 8 inches long.

Mix any remaining nuts and caramel, shape into squares and wrap in waxed paper.

## Divinity

    3 cups sugar
    3/4 cup light corn syrup
    3/4 cup water
    3 medium egg whites
    1/4 teaspoon salt
    1 teaspoon vanilla

Have the egg whites at room temperature. Before you start cooking the syrup, put the egg whites and salt in the large bowl of the mixer.

In a 2-quart saucepan, combine sugar, syrup and water. Bring to boil. Stir only until sugar is dissolved. Insert thermometer. Cook without stirring to 265 degrees. Remove from heat instantly and let stand while the egg whites are beaten. Beat only until foamy and clinging to sides of bowl—not stiff—about 2 minutes.

Now *slowly* pour the hot syrup over the eggs while the mixer beats at medium speed. Brace yourself to hold the pan a good while, for the syrup should be added in the tiniest stream. Otherwise, lumps may form.

Continue to beat until the mixture loses its gloss and becomes very heavy. Add vanilla. When the proper density is reached, drop by teaspoonfuls onto waxed paper in the usual way. Or: Pour out on oiled marble slab or platter and top with 2 squares unsweetened chocolate melted with 1 tablespoon butter. Cut in squares. Or: Pour onto oiled marble slab and spread with spatula to a ½-inch thickness.

Soften 1 cup crunchy peanut butter over warm water. Cut candy in half lengthwise. Spread both pieces with softened peanut butter and roll up like 2 jelly rolls. Slice to serve. Or wrap in waxed paper and refrigerate until needed. Makes 2 rolls 20 inches long.

# Come Fill the Cup!

Eggnog is the queen of beverages for holiday entertaining. Make it with straight bourbon, Kentucky style, or add some rum for a delicious variation. Punch is another useful item for entertaining a number of people, as is the old-fashioned wassail bowl.

## Kentucky-Georgetown Eggnog

6 eggs, separated
1 cup sugar
1 pint bourbon
1 quart heavy whipping cream

Separate eggs and beat yolks until light. Add 2/3-cup of the sugar and beat at least 5 minutes in mixer, or until frothy and lemon-colored. Then add bourbon, very, very slowly. If desired, ¼-cup rum may be combined with the bourbon.

Beat the egg whites until stiff, but not dry, with the remaining 1/3-cup sugar. Slowly pour the whisky-sugar-egg yolk mixture into the whites, folding it in gently to avoid separation.

Next, whip the cream and fold it into the eggnog. Fold several times and then let it stand; fold again several times and let stand again. Repeated folding and standing helps "ripen" a good eggnog. Eggnog should be made 2 to 3 days in advance, kept cool and stirred frequently.

## Bourbon Punch

1 pint iced tea (regular strength)
1 pint pineapple juice
1 quart orange juice
1 pint lemon juice
1 quart ginger ale
1 pint bourbon

Mix above ingredients. Make a simple syrup by boiling 2 cups sugar with a pint of water for 10 minutes; use to sweeten punch to taste.

## Citrus Wassail Bowl

4 Valencia oranges
1/2 cup lemon juice
Whole cloves
2 quarts sweet apple cider
Cinnamon sticks

Stud the oranges with the whole cloves, spacing about ¼-inch apart. Place oranges in shallow pan, set in 350-degree oven for 30 minutes. Heat cider just below boiling point and add lemon juice. Pour into heat-proof punch bowl. Pierce baked oranges with ice pick, add to hot cider. Ladle hot cider over oranges. Serve in mugs using cinnamon sticks for stirring. Makes 10 to 12 servings.

## Cocktail Punch

1 quart bourbon
1 pint lemon juice
1 cup simple syrup
1 pint club soda
Assorted sliced fruits

Blend the first 3 ingredients, chill in the refrigerator or freezer. Just before serving add club soda and assorted sliced fruits. Makes about 12 servings.

## Festive Citrus Tea

Grated peel of a thick-skinned orange
Grated peel of one lemon
3 sticks crushed stick cinnamon
20 whole cloves
4 quarts cold water
3 tablespoons black tea
Juice of 8 oranges
Juice of 4 lemons
2 cups pineapple juice
About 1 1/2 cups sugar (to taste)

Tie fruit peel and spices in cloth bag. Place in water and bring to a boil. Let stand overnight. Remove spice bag and bring to a boil. Put in tea for 5 minutes. Add juices and sugar. Reheat to boiling point. Serve hot or cold. Serves 20 to 25.

## Party Tea Punch

1 tablespoon tea leaves
3/4 cup freshly boiled water
1/2 cup sugar
1/3 cup boiling water
Juice of 3 oranges
Juice of 2 lemons
1/3 cup chopped pineapple
1/3 cup raspberry syrup (use frozen raspberries, defrosted, sieved and resweetened to taste)
Food coloring (optional)
1 pint club soda
1 pint lemon sherbet

Make tea using the 2 first ingredients. Strain and chill. Combine sugar and water and boil gently 5 minutes. Chill. Combine chilled tea, syrup, orange and lemon juices, chopped pineapple and raspberry syrup. Tint with food coloring, if desired. Just before serving, add chilled club soda and lemon sherbet. Serve in punch glasses. 14 servings.

# A Legendary Cake

Cissy Gregg's Kentucky Bourbon Pecan Cake is the standard by which others are measured. You may decorate before baking, as directed in the recipe, or you may decorate it after it is baked, as shown in the picture, for even more sumptuous effect.

### Kentucky Pecan Bourbon Cake

1 pound shelled pecans
1/2 cup butter
3 eggs, separated
1 1/2 cups flour
1 teaspoon baking powder
1 cup, plus 2 tablespoons sugar
1/2 pound seeded raisins
2 teaspoons freshly grated nutmeg
1/2 cup (4 ounces) bonded Kentucky bourbon
Jumbo pecan halves and candied cherries for decorating top of cake

Break the pecans in pieces with the fingers or chop very coarsely; cut the raisins in half; set aside. Measure the flour after sifting once, then sift twice more. Take ½ cup of this flour and mix with the nuts and raisins. To the rest of the flour add the baking powder and sift again. Cream butter and sugar. Add yolks of eggs 1 at a time, beating until mixture is smooth and lemon-colored.

Soak the nutmeg in the bourbon for at least 10 minutes, then add to the butter-and-egg mixture, alternating with the flour, and beating as the batter is being blended. When finished, it looks and tastes a great deal like eggnog. Slowly fold the raisins and nuts into the batter, using a heavy wooden or large metal spoon. Beat the egg whites until stiff, with a few grains of salt. Fold egg whites into batter. Grease a metal tube pan large enough to hold 3 pounds of batter. Line it with brown paper, greased on both sides. After filling the pan with the batter let it stand for 10 minutes.

Meantime, decorate the top of the cake with the candied cherries and jumbo pecan halves. Bake at 325 degrees for 1¼ hours, but if the top browns too quickly put a piece of heavy wrapping paper over it.

Test the cake by pressing the surface of the dough with the fingers. If it seems firm and the indentation does not show, the cake is done. It should always be slightly moist, so even though a few crumbs may adhere in a straw test the cake is ready to take out of the oven.

Let the cake stand 30 minutes before trying to remove it from the pan. Then place a plate over the surface and quickly turn the pan upside down. Then carefully turn the cake right side up on another plate; being watchful not to disturb the decorations on top. Cut with a saw-edged knife as it crumbles easily.

Coffee goes well with cake, and so does the following cranberry drink.

### Cranberry Drink

1 pint cranberries
1 pint water
3 cloves
1/2 stick cinnamon
1 cup sugar, or to taste
1/4 cup orange juice
1 tablespoon lemon juice

Place the cleaned cranberries in a saucepan with water and spices. Cook until the fruit is very soft. Strain. Add sugar to the juice and simmer, stirring until the sugar is dissolved. Cool. Add orange and lemon juice and chill. Serves 4.

# Christmas Dinner

If you treasure Christmas traditions but feel loosely bound by them, forsake the old ham and turkey routine and make a glorious spiced round of beef for Christmas dinner. It takes time, eight days for a 15-pound round, 11 days for a 30-pound piece. But it is a never-to-be-forgotten treat, once you've done it!

## Hot Shrimp in Wine

Water to boil shrimp
1 lemon slice
1 teaspoon salt
1 bay leaf
A bit of onion
2 pounds fresh or frozen shrimp
1/2 stick butter
1 teaspoon dried tarragon
1 1/2 tablespoons minced fresh parsley
1/2 teaspoon salt
1/4 teaspoon white pepper
1/2 cup dry bread crumbs
1/4 cup vermouth or other dry white wine

Shell fresh shrimp. Bring a kettle of water to boiling and add to it lemon slice, teaspoon salt, bay leaf and the bit of onion. Drop in the shrimp and boil 3 minutes. If frozen shrimps are used, prepare them according to package directions, but undercook them slightly. Drain and place shrimp in a buttered, shallow baking dish.

Using a pastry blender or the fingers, blend the butter, tarragon, parsley, salt, pepper and bread crumbs until the mixture is like coarse crumbs. Sprinkle over shrimp. Pour wine down side of baking dish so it covers the bottom.

Five minutes before serving, put under broiler till brown and bubbly. 8 servings.

## Spiced Round of Beef

Large round of beef, at least 15 pounds, of fine quality
2 ounces powdered saltpeter (10 teaspoons)
5 teaspoons powdered mace
1 cup salt
1 tablespoon nutmeg
1 tablespoon pepper
3 teaspoons powdered cloves
Sweet herbs (basil and marjoram)
1/2 pound light brown sugar
1/2 pound beef suet

Have butcher bone and tie the beef round tightly to hold its shape through the processing. Rub meat all over with saltpeter. Place in enamel or crockery container (a refrigerator vegetable drawer), cover tightly and set in a cool place, or refrigerate, for 2 days.

Rub the salt into the meat and return it to the container for 5 or 6 days, turning the piece over daily. At the end of that time, blend mace, nutmeg, pepper, cloves and brown sugar together and rub well into the meat. Fill the hole where the bone was with crushed sweet herbs, packing them in loosely.

Divide the suet into 2 parts and flatten or slice thin. Put half under the meat in roasting pan, the other half over the top. Wrap the entire bundle in cheesecloth just to make sure it keeps its shape. Lay a sheet of foil over the top and put a large, heavy, heatproof plate over all. Roast in 325-degree oven for 3 hours or until meat thermometer reads 160 degrees (medium). The temperature will continue to rise somewhat after it comes from the oven. Let rest 30 minutes before carving. Good served cold, too.

## Chestnut Mold

2 pounds chestnuts
3/4 cup sugar
4 eggs
4 ounces sweet chocolate, shaved or grated
1/4 teaspoon salt
2 cups light cream
2 teaspoons vanilla
6 tablespoons rum or cognac (optional)
1 1/2 cups heavy cream, whipped
1/4 cup powdered sugar
For garnish: 1/2 square of unsweetened chocolate, shaved into curls

Cut a slit in each chestnut and boil 40 to 45 minutes, until meat is very soft. Cool enough to handle and remove shells and brown inner skins. Purée by putting a few at a time in a blender or forcing through a food mill.

In the top of a double boiler, beat the eggs with the salt and sugar. Place over hot (not boiling) water and add the light cream and the chocolate. Stir and cook until chocolate is melted and mixture will coat a metal spoon. Add 4 tablespoons of the rum or cognac and the vanilla to the chestnut pureé. (If not using the spirits, you may want to increase the vanilla to 3 teaspoons.) Blend the chestnut pureé with the hot-custard mixture. Cool.

Butter a 9-inch spring-form pan or a 9-inch tube pan and pour in the mixture. Chill overnight. To serve, unmold onto a serving plate. Whip the cream and add the remaining 2 tablespoons rum or cognac and the powdered sugar, blending well. Spread over cake and decorate with curls of unsweetened chocolate. 16 servings.

# INDEX

Design and Sketches by Robin Briggs

Production Editor, Milli Hamilton

Photograph Credit:

H. Harold Davis
Pages 1, 9, 11, 12, 14, 22, 24, 29, 34, 37, 38, 40, 42,
52, 55, 58, 63, 65, 67, 68, 73, 74, 83, 84, 90, 92, 99,
101, 102, 104, 109, 116, 119, 124, 130, 135, 136, 141,
144, 147, 148.

Carl Rainbolt
Pages 5, 7, 18, 19, 31, 32, 45, 49, 50, 57, 61, 70, 78,
79, 86, 89, 94, 97, 106, 110, 113, 115, 121, 127, 129,
133, 139.

R. C. Fuller
Page 123.

A Publication of

# Pegasus

## A Service for Newspapers
Louisville, Kentucky 40202